A TASTE OF SUMMER

by Brian Turner

A collection of delicious Summer recipes

BUCKINGHAM
BOOK PUBLISHING LTD

First published in 2011
by Buckingham Book Publishing Ltd.
Network House, 28 Ballmoor, Celtic Court,
Buckingham MK18 1RQ, UK
www.chefmagazine.co.uk

ISBN 978-0-9567667-5-5
Printed in China by CT Printing Ltd.

Publisher: Peter Marshall
Author: Brian Turner
Managing Editor: Shirley Marshall
Editor: Katy Morris
Recipe Editor: Sue Christelow
Design Director: Philip Donnelly
Recipe photography: Myburgh du Plessis

Recipe ingredients may vary slightly from picture shown.

Knowing Brian is a privilege; his kindness and skills as a chef are among his many attributes.

In his new book A Taste of Summer Brian is loyal to himself, he is not pretending to be one thing and offering another. You will find a festival of over 90 summer recipes in the book, using only seasonal products, and unusually for these days, only a few ingredients are called for in each one, so you won't need to spend half a day buying the ingredients!

The pleasure keeps on coming, as the dishes take so little time to prepare that you will have plenty of time to enjoy one of the summer cocktail recipes included in the book.

This is my favourite summer book – tasty recipes and mouthwatering photography, I recommend you keep an eye on it as everyone will want to enjoy it – my dear wife Robyn has already pinched my copy!

Happy cooking and happy eating with Brian!

Michel Roux OBE

Michel

Contents

Scorching summer days and never-ending warm summer nights,

for me there is nothing better than enjoying the flavours of summer outside on a patio or on freshly mowed green grass. Summer is just the season of relaxation – long days, short sleeves, warm but mild breezes that refresh and soothe and above all that feeling of holidays – when even evenings are worshipped as a small opportunity to enjoy the great outdoors.

When anybody asks about how I enjoy my summers I can't help but think back to my days as a child – holidays would be the memory of choice, school holidays definitely but more the memory of trips to the Great British seaside, Scarborough, Filey and Brid, the smell and warm weather of the Yorkshire dales and the good mood that everyone shares when in good weather.

One thing that really strikes me in the summer months is that everyone is more likely to let go a little bit – I don't just enjoy good food on my summer holiday but in my summer in general. It is just the perfect time for whatever you like best.

In this book I have included summer staples such as salads and barbecues but also classic dishes with a summer twist. Stews and roasted dishes also feature in this book, after all many of the hottest countries in the world enjoy this food as their day-to-day meal. And as much as we plan for good weather the great British summer can sometimes be a bit of a washout, so it's good to have some warming recipes on standby!

As well as tasty and easy-to-make foods this book also includes a classic cocktail section, kindly prepared by my friends at The Waterside Inn. These are simple-to-prepare drinks that don't require tons of ingredients but are perfect to impress guests or just to enjoy on a relaxing summer evening. Tangy homemade lemonade or fruity punch are great after a day outside with the kids.

All the dishes and drinks in this book are designed not only with flavour in mind but for that ultimate holiday feeling of pushing the boat out and trying something new. My favourite of these dishes is the pan-fried lambs' liver which is not only extremely healthy but quick, inexpensive and equally as tasty.

So go on, try it – there's no better time than summer to try something new.

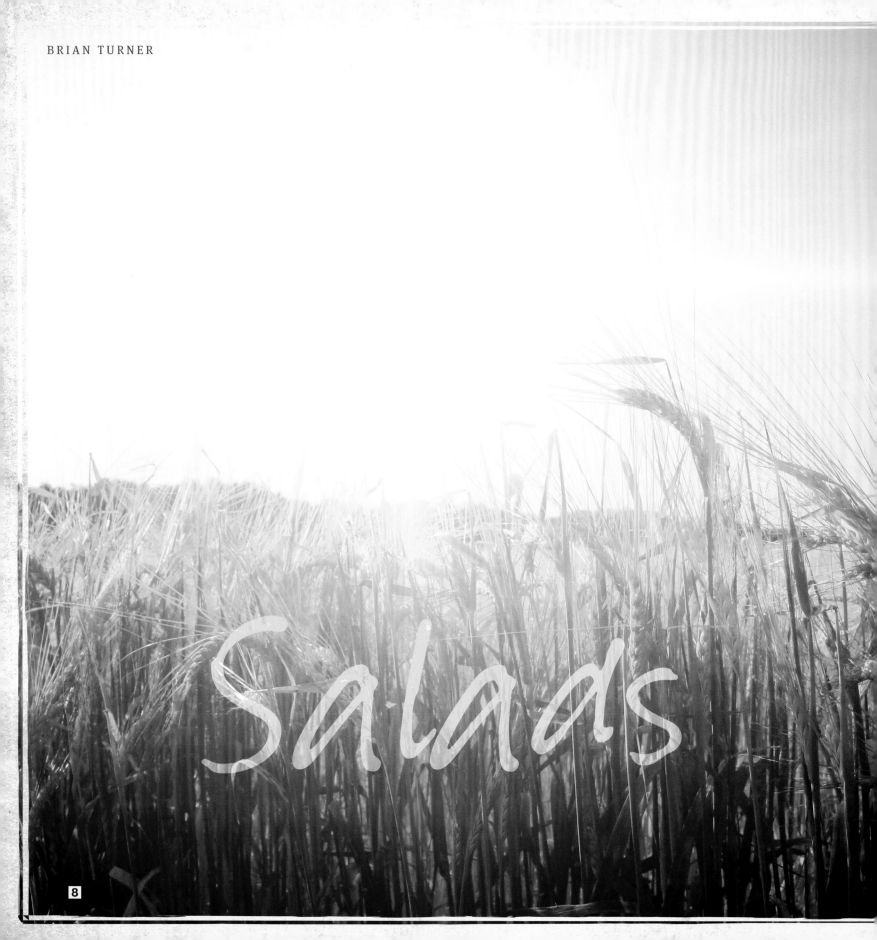

Salads

Salads

An automatic choice for many in summertime due to the light but full feeling that a good salad provides. The best thing about salads is that you can make them as simple or as complex as you like with the addition of fresh meats, fish or cheese. Fresh and crispy cos lettuce dressed with a basic vinaigrette is a fantastic dish, just keep tasting your dressing in order to get the right balance of flavours and mix well for a good consistency. The recipe for the crab salad is a stunner – crab is a really succulent meat and this dish works fantastically with the sweetness of the melon.

Asparagus, mustard and herb salad with a radish dressing

SERVES 4

HOW TO CREATE THE DISH

- Cook the asparagus in boiling salted water. When cooked take out and plunge into iced water.
- Take out and drain.
- Cut the tips into 7.5cm pieces and the rest of the stalks into 2.5cm pieces.
- Put the 2.5cm asparagus pieces into a bowl and add the chervil, chives, parsley, tarragon and basil, then mix together.
- In a separate bowl mix the mustard, lemon juice and oil, then season.
- Cut the radishes into 3mm batons and put into the dressing.
- Add three-quarters of the dressing to the herb mix and season.
- Put the herbs/dressing onto four plates.
- Lay the asparagus tips on top and then pour the remaining dressing over the top and serve.

Fresh asparagus

Carrot salad with mint, orange and garlic dressing

SERVES 4

SHOPPING LIST

450g carrots, peeled
2 tbsp fresh orange juice
Zest of 1 orange
½ garlic clove, crushed
1 tbsp lemon juice
3 tbsp olive oil
1 tbsp chopped mint
Salt & pepper
2 oranges, in segments

HOW TO CREATE THE DISH

- Grate the peeled carrots in a large grater.
- Plunge into boiling salted water then take out and cool in iced water.
- Drain and dry.
- Mix the orange juice, zest, garlic and lemon juice together then add the carrots and mix well.
- Just before serving add the olive oil and mint, and season.
- Garnish with orange segments and serve.

Carrots

Celeriac remoulade

SERVES 4–6

SHOPPING LIST

4 tbsp mayonnaise

4 tbsp crème fraîche

2 tbsp chopped gherkins

1 tbsp Dijon mustard

1 tbsp chopped tarragon

1 tbsp chopped parsley

Salt

Pinch of cayenne pepper

2 anchovy fillets, chopped

1 small celeriac

Juice of ½ lemon

HOW TO CREATE THE DISH

- Mix the mayonnaise and crème fraîche with the gherkins, mustard, tarragon and parsley.
- Add salt and cayenne to taste, then the anchovies.
- Put into the fridge for 2 hours.
- Peel the celeriac then, using a mandoline cutter, cut into thin strips 3mm thick.
- Put these into a bowl, add the lemon juice and then half of the sauce and leave to marinate overnight.
- Add more sauce, mix well and serve.

PS
- This dish can be served as a starter, but it is often served as an accompaniment to cold meats, such as smoked chicken, roast chicken or roast pork. It also works as a dip for crudités or goujons of fish.

Celeriac

Classic tuna salade niçoise

SERVES 4

HOW TO CREATE THE DISH

- Carefully add to the tuna the first shallot, capers, parsley and tarragon. Mix with a fork.
- Chop the anchovy fillets and add to the shallot mix with the mustard, vinegar and oil. Season and stir well.
- Cut the cleaned little gem lettuces in half vertically.
- Spoon 1tbsp of dressing over the lettuces and season.
- Put 1tbsp of dressing into the beans and add the other shallot, season and put in the bottom of a bowl.
- Spoon the tuna mix on top.
- Cut the eggs and tomatoes in quarters and arrange over the tuna.
- Add the spring onions, parsley and olives to the remainder of the dressing.
- Pour over the tuna and serve.

Olives

Cricket

Summer is the sound of willow on wood in sleepy country villages

Crab meat and melon salad

SERVES 4

SHOPPING LIST

350g fresh white crab meat

1tbsp chopped dill

Squeeze of lemon juice

Salt & pepper

1tsp pommery mustard

1tbsp white wine vinegar

3tbsp olive oil

110g baby spinach

50g lambs lettuce

1 small sweet melon, chilled

HOW TO CREATE THE DISH

- Mix the crab meat, dill and lemon juice, and season.
- Leave to marinate.
- Mix the mustard with the vinegar, add the oil and season.
- Toss the spinach and lambs lettuce in the dressing and check the seasoning.
- Cut the melon in half lengthwise and remove the skin. Take out the seeds and slice wafer thin.
- Arrange the melon around the edge of the plate.
- Carefully lay the mixed leaves in the middle.
- Sprinkle the crab meat on top.
- Decorate with the melon and serve.

Melon

Flaked salmon, boiled egg, cos lettuce, new potatoes and tomato dressing

SERVES 4

1 splash olive oil

6 over-ripe tomatoes, chopped

1 clove garlic, crushed

1 pinch oregano

1 pinch sugar

Salt & pepper

1tsp Dijon mustard

2tbsp white wine vinegar

8tbsp olive oil

2 heads cos lettuce

12 cooked new potatoes, quartered

480g poached salmon, flaked

4 soft-boiled eggs (6 minutes), halved

4 ripe tomatoes, each cut into 6

Seasonal baby salad leaves

HOW TO CREATE THE DISH

- Heat the olive oil then add the chopped ripe tomatoes and garlic.
- Cook until very soft, then add the oregano and sugar, and season.
- Liquidise and allow to cool.
- Mix the Dijon mustard with the white wine vinegar and olive oil and season, then add the tomato mixture to make the dressing.
- Separate and wash the cos lettuce leaves and put into a bowl.
- Add the potatoes and flaked salmon along with half of the dressing.
- Place this on plates, decorate with boiled egg halves and tomatoes.
- Decorate with the seasonal leaves and more dressing.

Soft-boiled eggs

Green bean salad with olives, cherry tomatoes and citrus dressing

SERVES 4

SHOPPING LIST

- 100g fine French beans
- 100g haricot blanc (white beans)
- 100g cannellini beans
- 100g broad beans
- 100g pitted black olives
- 200g red & yellow cherry tomatoes
- 1tsp Dijon mustard
- 1tbsp cider vinegar
- Juice of 1 lemon
- Zest of 1 lemon
- 8tbsp olive oil
- Salt & pepper
- 1 iceberg lettuce
- Seasonal baby salad leaves

HOW TO CREATE THE DISH

White beans

- Cook all the beans separately and refresh, then drain.
- Cut the French beans into 1cm pieces.
- Mix all the beans together and add the olives.
- Cut the cherry tomatoes in half and add to the beans.
- Whisk the Dijon mustard, cider vinegar and lemon juice together.
- Add the zest of lemon, then whisk in the olive oil and season.
- Put 1tbsp dressing into the tomato and bean mix, and season.
- Tear the iceberg lettuce and lay in a bowl.
- Spoon the bean mixture over the top.
- Decorate with the baby salad leaves.
- Pour the rest of the dressing over and serve.

Pea, courgette, cucumber, spring onion and asparagus salad, on little gem leaf with a radish dressing

SERVES 4

SHOPPING LIST

2 courgettes

175g peas

8 asparagus

2 spring onions

½ cucumber

8 little gem leaves

6 radishes

1tsp grain mustard

Juice of 1 lemon

4tbsp groundnut oil

4tbsp olive oil

1tbsp chopped chives

Salt & pepper

HOW TO CREATE THE DISH

- Cut the courgettes into 6mm dice and blanche for 2-3 minutes with the peas. Refresh in cold water and drain.
- Cook the asparagus, trim 4cm from the tops and chop the stems, keep the tips apart.
- Cut the spring onions into 6mm lengths, then add to a bowl with the asparagus stalks, peas and courgettes.
- Cut the cucumber into 6mm dice and mix in.
- Shred half of the lettuce leaves and put to one side.
- Cut the radishes into fine dice and put into a separate bowl.
- Add the mustard and lemon juice, and mix well.
- Stir in the oils then the chives and season.
- Add some dressing without radish to the vegetable mixture.
- Lay shredded lettuce into the remaining leaves on each serving dish.
- Spoon the vegetable mixture on top.
- Garnish with two spears of asparagus on each.
- Spoon the radish dressing over and around, and serve.

Gem leaf

Roasted breast of quail on a Waldorf salad with a green apple dressing

SERVES **4**

HOW TO CREATE THE DISH

- Shred the basil leaves and mix with the walnut oil.
- Brush the quail skins with the basil/walnut mix and sear.
- Brush regularly with the basil/walnut mix.
- Add the mirepoix to a roasting dish.
- Stand the quail crown on top, season and roast in the oven at 200°C for 8-10 minutes, keep pink.
- Take out of the oven and out of the dish and keep warm.
- Meanwhile clean the green apples, cut a thin 3mm slice and cut into dice. Put into lemon juice.
- Cut the rest of the apples into small batons and place into the mayonnaise, add the crème fraîche, cut the radishes to the same size and add.
- Peel and cut the celery into same-size batons and add to the mix.
- Break up the walnuts and add.
- Mix and check the seasoning.
- Spoon into the middle of each bowl.
- Mix the green dice of apple and lemon juice with the olive oil and season with the tabasco.
- Take off the quail breasts and lay on the salad.
- Spoon the dressing over, lay the chervil on top and serve.

Green apples

Salad of breast of chicken with avocado, cherry tomatoes and herb dressing

SERVES 4

SHOPPING LIST

50g butter

2 crowns of roasting chickens

Salt & pepper

8tbsp olive oil

1tsp Dijon mustard

2tbsp white wine vinegar

Mixed seasonal baby salad leaves

150g cherry tomatoes, cut as desired

1 bunch picked chervil

1 bunch chives cut in 2.5cm pieces

2tbsp chopped parsley

2 avocado pears

HOW TO CREATE THE DISH

- Melt the butter in a roasting tray.
- Colour the crowns of chicken, season and roast at 180°C for 30-40 minutes until cooked.
- When ready take out and keep warm.
- Make a vinaigrette dressing with the olive oil, Dijon mustard and white wine vinegar, and season.
- In a bowl combine the baby salad leaves, cut tomatoes and herbs then dress with three-quarters of the vinaigrette.
- Put the dressed salad in the centre of the plate.

- Take the breasts off the bone and lay on top of the salad.
- Stone, skin and slice the avocado and dress round the plate.
- Pour the rest of the vinaigrette over the avocado and serve.

Olive oil

Salad of spiced Gloucestershire Old Spot

SERVES 4

SHOPPING LIST

2 fillets of Old Spot, 450g total

Olive oil, as required

½ red chilli

1 clove garlic

1 stalk lemongrass

1cm ginger

Salt & pepper

½tsp soy sauce

Salt & pepper

1 red apple

1 celery stick

12 walnut halves

Curly endive

Lambs lettuce

150ml vinaigrette

½ bunch tarragon

1 tbsp chopped parsley

HOW TO CREATE THE DISH

- Seal and colour the outsides of the pork in the oil and leave to cool.
- Chop the spices together, add salt and mix with the soy sauce.
- Smear over the fillets of pork, wrap tightly in cling film and put in the fridge for 12 hours.
- When ready to use roast in the oven at 220°C for 10-12 minutes.

- Meanwhile cut the apple and celery into equal sized batons, mix together and break the walnuts into the mixture.
- Tear the endive into the mixture then add the lambs lettuce, season and add 2 tbsp vinaigrette.
- Strip the tarragon and mix the leaves into the salad.
- Slice the pork and lay in a circle round the outside of the plates.
- Mix the salad and lay in the middle of the plate.
- Dribble the rest of the vinaigrette mixed with the parsley round the outside and over the meat, then serve.

Walnuts

Canalling

A Taste of Summer with Brian Turner

Summer is when time stands still on leisurely taken canal journeys

Scallop and bean salad with a raisin dressing

SERVES **4**

HOW TO CREATE THE DISH

- Soak 25g raisins in the brandy.
- Purée in a machine and put into a bowl.
- Add the olive oil and whisk in.
- Add the lime juice and parsley, and season.
- Cut the radishes into batons 3mm square.
- Cut the cucumber into 2.5cm lengths then into 3mm batons around the seeds.
- Mix with the radishes.
- Cut the beans into 2.5cm lengths and mix with the dill, yoghurt and 50g raisins, then with the radish and cucumber, and season.
- Sear the scallops in hot oil and then season.
- Lay four little gem leaves on each plate.
- Place the bean mix into the centre of the leaves.
- Lay the scallops on top.
- Decorate with the dressing and serve.

Raisins

Tomato salad

SERVES 4

SHOPPING LIST

16 cherry tomatoes
Salt & pepper
1tbsp olive oil
1tsp balsamic vinegar
1 sprig fresh oregano
4 tomatoes
1tbsp cider vinegar
3tbsp olive oil
2 shallots

HOW TO CREATE THE DISH

- Cut the cherry tomatoes in half and lay on a roasting tray.
- Sprinkle with salt and pepper, 1tbsp olive oil, the balsamic vinegar and sprig of oregano.
- Put into the oven at 160°C and leave for 10 minutes.
- Take out and allow to cool.
- Meanwhile take the green core out of the tomatoes and slice across the tomato.
- Lay the sliced tomato on the plate in a circular shape.
- Pile the roasted tomatoes in the middle of the sliced tomatoes.
- Mix the cider vinegar and 3tbsp olive oil and season the mixture.
- Shred the shallots.
- Mix the residue of juice from roasting the tomatoes with the dressing.
- Spoon over the tomato salad.
- Sprinkle the shallots over and serve.

Tomatoes

Roast baby beet, potato and blue cheese salad

SERVES 4

SHOPPING LIST

6 baby beetroot

3tbsp olive oil

1tbsp red wine vinegar

1tsp brown sugar

450g baby new potatoes

110g Yorkshire blue cheese

1tbsp olive oil

2tbsp walnut oil

2tbsp toasted walnuts, chopped

Sea salt & pepper

HOW TO CREATE THE DISH

- Cut the beetroot in half lengthways, lay on a tray and drizzle with 3tbsp oil, vinegar and sugar.
- Roast in the oven at 180°C for 30-40 minutes until tender.
- Cook the potatoes in boiling salted water for 20 minutes till tender, drain well and cut in half.
- Put into a bowl with the beets and crumble the cheese over.
- Sprinkle with the oils, add the walnuts, season and serve.

PS

- You can use boiled beets as well, just roast for less time.

Blue cheese

Warm goat's cheese on a green bean, watercress and hazelnut salad

SERVES 4

350g haricot verts (green) beans

2 bunches watercress

75g hazelnuts

1tsp Dijon mustard

1tsp red wine vinegar

2tsp olive oil

2tbsp groundnut oil

Salt & pepper

4 x 2.5cm thick slices of goat's cheese log (6.5cm diameter)

Splash of olive oil

HOW TO CREATE THE DISH

- Pick the green beans and plunge into boiling salted water.
- Cook then put into cold water to refresh, then strain and drain.
- Pick over the watercress to remove excess stalks and mix with the beans.
- Heat a pan, add the hazelnuts and roast gently, put into a coffee grinder and blitz into a chunky powder then mix with the beans and watercress.

- Mix the mustard with the vinegar, add the olive oil and groundnut oil and season.
- Put the slices of cheese on a tray.
- Splash with olive oil and put under the grill.
- Mix the dressing with the salad and then put onto the plates.
- Place the grilled cheese on top and serve.

PS

- I love soft English goat's cheese.

Goat's cheese

Soups & Starters

Soups & Starters

Soup is not a dish that most associate with the summer months but it is a perfect option for a light meal in the evenings when the days are warm or chilled as a refreshing midday meal. Full of nutrients and packed full of taste soup is a quick and easy alternative to full dishes and great when the Great British weather is a little unreliable. Serve with bread or as a starter before a salad for an extra course. For those wanting a light bite the starters in this section fit the bill nicely. The creamed mushrooms on toast are a delightful lunch or starter with the full flavour of the mushrooms really coming through.

Avocado and coconut soup

SERVES 4

HOW TO CREATE THE DISH

- Peel and stone the avocados and put into a liquidiser.
- Add the coconut milk, chicken stock and crushed garlic.
- Top, tail and deseed the chilli, chop and add to the liquidiser with the lemon juice and season with salt.
- Purée the mix.
- Put into a bowl and chill for 4 hours.
- Check the seasoning and put into serving bowls.
- Mix the spring onions with the chopped parsley and olive oil.
- Swirl on top of the soup and serve.

Avocados

Celery and Wensleydale cream soup

SERVES 4–6

HOW TO CREATE THE DISH

- Melt the 50g butter in a pan, add the 275g celery and onion and sweat, but do not colour.
- Add the potato and cook for 2 minutes, then add the stock and season lightly.
- Cook for 30 minutes.
- Put into a food processor then pass through a sieve into a clean pan and bring up to the boil.
- Meanwhile for the garnish melt the butter, add the celery and cook, but do not colour.
- Mix the double cream, egg yolks and cheese.
- Pour the hot soup over, put back into the pan and reheat – do not boil.
- Test for seasoning and serve. Sprinkle with the celery leaves and parsley.

Celery

Chilled cucumber and green pepper soup

SERVES 4

SHOPPING LIST

450g cucumber
4 green peppers
1 green chilli
1 tsp toasted caraway seeds
2 tbsp mint leaves
Salt, to taste
225g natural yoghurt

Green peppers

- Peel and deseed the cucumber.
- Deseed the green peppers.
- Top, tail and deseed the chilli.
- Put all into a liquidiser with the caraway seeds and purée.
- Add the mint leaves and salt and liquidise.
- Finally add the yoghurt, then check the seasoning.
- Chill in the fridge for 4 hours then serve.

Creamed mushrooms on toast

SERVES 4

650g button mushrooms
Juice of ½ lemon, freshly squeezed
50g unsalted butter
2 shallots, finely chopped
80ml dry sherry
300ml double cream
Salt & pepper
1tbsp chopped parsley
4 slices sourdough bread

HOW TO CREATE THE DISH

- Cut the mushrooms into quarters.
- Mix with the fresh lemon juice.
- Melt the butter, add the shallots and sweat, do not colour, then add the mushrooms and cook for 2 minutes.
- Add the sherry and reduce to a syrup.
- Add the double cream and reduce until it coats the mushrooms.
- Season, add the parsley and serve on toasted sourdough bread.

Button mushrooms

Gazpacho with cockles

SERVES 4

SHOPPING LIST

450g cockles
75ml dry white wine
450g ripe tomatoes
1 pepper, deseeded
½ cucumber
1 small onion
1 clove garlic
Salt & pepper
2 slices day-old bread, crusts off
2tbsp red wine vinegar
150ml cold water
2tbsp olive oil
300ml tomato passata

GARNISH:
1 baguette style loaf of bread
Olive oil
1tbsp chopped parsley

HOW TO CREATE THE DISH

- Put the cockles in a pan with the white wine with a lid on until the cockles are opened.
- Drain off the cockles and strain the liquor.
- Put in the fridge and allow to cool.
- Pick out the cockles and keep in the fridge.
- Meanwhile chop the tomatoes, pepper, cucumber, onion and garlic roughly and mix together, then add salt and pepper. Leave to marinate overnight.
- Put the bread with the vinegar and cold water to soak.
- Liquidise the vegetables.
- Whisk the bread, vinegar, cold water and cockle juice together then add to the liquidised vegetables with the olive oil. Whisk in the tomato passata and check the seasoning.

- Put in the fridge and serve chilled.
- For the garnish, cut the baguette into slices, sprinkle with olive oil and toast.
- Season the cockles and add the parsley.
- Serve the soup in bowls, add the toasted bread then sprinkle the cockles on top.

Cockles

Lawns

Summer is taking pleasure in lovingly tended lawns at home and on the sporting field

A Taste of Summer with Brian Turner

A Taste of Summer with Brian Turner

Green pea and ham soup

Pea soup was also known as 'London particular', which referred to the
London smog of the fifties known as a 'Pea souper'. This was because of
the thickness of pea soup, made probably with dried peas and laboriously
in those days passed through a sieve. There are so many versions of pea
soup that to say one is the definitive classical recipe for Pea & Ham is
practically impossible, soup made from tinned peas is my least favourite,
but made from dried, fresh or a mixture work great. However, this is my
favourite version made in a classical style and will always remind me of
the time Bob Holness came on 'Ready Steady Cook' and I made him some
pea soup which allowed the lovable Fern Britton to utter those immortal
lines 'Can I have a 'P' please, Bob?'

Green pea and ham soup

SERVES 8

HOW TO CREATE THE DISH

SHOPPING LIST

1 ham hock

4.5 litres water

2 whole carrots, peeled

2 whole onions, peeled

1 head celery, washed

12 peppercorns

1 bay leaf

75g butter

1 small onion, finely diced

900g frozen peas

1 small bunch mint

75g flour

1.8 litres ham stock (reserved from earlier)

300ml double cream

Salt & pepper

- Soak the hock for 12 hours then add it to the cold water in a pan, bring to the boil and skim off any scum.
- Add the carrots, onions and celery.
- Leave gently to simmer, adding the peppercorns and bay leaf, and cook for 2-2½ hours until the ham is cooked through.
- Strain off the stock for the soup and reserve.
- Melt the butter in heavy-bottomed pan, add the onion and 450g frozen peas.
- Add the mint, tied with string, and put a lid on the pan and allow to gently stew for 3-5 minutes.
- At this point add the flour and stir in carefully, possibly taking the pan off the heat to stop it sticking.
- Put the pan back on the heat and cook the pea 'roux' for 2 minutes, but do not colour.
- Slowly add the hot strained ham stock, beating well with a wooden spoon after each addition to get rid of any lumps of flour.
- When the stock is all added make sure that the bottom of the pan is clear of everything, then leave to simmer for 20 minutes.
- Meanwhile blanch the rest of the peas in boiling water for just 2 minutes and then take them out and plunge into a bowl of iced water – this will retain the colour of the peas.
- At the same time it is a good idea to take the skin from the ham hock, to take the meat from the bone and to carefully cut it into fine dice.
- Mix this ham with half of the blanched peas and keep to one side.
- The soup is now cooked so take out the bunch of mint and put the remaining blanched peas into the soup.
- Liquidise the soup in a machine and then I like to push this through a fine sieve or chinoise (a conical strainer).
- When all is through reboil the soup gently, adding the double cream and adjusting the seasoning as necessary.
- Put the peas and ham into the soup and serve immediately.

PS

- Pea soup is not traditionally served with ham in it but this addition makes a 'gutsy' dish. Pea soup is often served with toasted bread triangles but I prefer it with croutons, i.e. a dice of fried bread. Pea soup is great chilled with perhaps extra cream and chopped mint. The French serve stewed lettuce and baby onions with their pea soup.

Jerusalem artichoke and mussel cream soup

SERVES 8

SHOPPING LIST

110g butter
2 shallots, chopped
2 cloves garlic, finely chopped
½ leek, finely chopped
700g Jerusalem artichokes
1.2 litres mussels, cleaned
300ml dry white wine
1.2 litres chicken stock
Salt & pepper
600ml double cream
2 tbsp chives, chopped

- Melt the butter in a pan.
- Add half the shallots, all the garlic and leek and sweat, but do not colour.
- Peel the artichokes then wash and chop and add to the shallots and garlic.
- Cover with a lid and gently cook for 10 minutes until soft.

- Meanwhile put the rest of the shallots, mussels and wine into another pan, cover and open up the mussels.
- Take the mussels out and put to one side.
- Strain add the cooking liquor then the chicken stock to the artichokes.
- Take the mussels from the shells, keep enough for garnish and put the rest into the soup.
- Liquidise well and pass through a chinoise into a clean pan, season and add the double cream.
- Reboil until the correct consistency.
- Put the mussels into the soup cups and add the chives.
- Pour the soup over and serve.

Jerusalem artichokes

Macaroni cheese with slow-cooked cherry tomatoes

SERVES 4

SHOPPING LIST

200g red cherry tomatoes

2tbsp olive oil

2 cloves garlic, crushed

1tbsp oregano

Salt & pepper

100g macaroni (2cm tube size)

50g butter

1 finely chopped onion

25g plain flour

200ml full-fat milk

200ml double cream

200g grated mature cheddar cheese

1 egg yolk

50g grated parmesan

HOW TO CREATE THE DISH

- Cut the tomatoes in half and lay on a tray.
- Sprinkle with the olive oil, garlic, oregano and season.
- Cook in a slow oven at 100°C for 30 minutes.
- Meanwhile, cook the macaroni in boiling salted water, drain and put to one side.
- Melt the butter and add the chopped onion.
- Sweat, but do not colour.
- Add the flour, stir well and cook for 1 minute, do not colour.
- Slowly add the milk and cream and whisk in to avoid lumps.
- Beat smooth and remove from the heat.
- Add the grated cheddar and season, then add the egg yolk and the macaroni to reheat.
- Put into serving dishes with tomatoes underneath.
- Sprinkle with parmesan and colour well under a grill to serve and put tomatoes on top.

Macaroni

New potato and leek chowder

SERVES 4

HOW TO CREATE THE DISH

- Carefully wash and clean the leeks.
- Shred and add to the melted butter.
- Add a quarter of the potatoes washed and thinly sliced and sweat without colour for 5 minutes.
- Add the flour and stir in well.
- Add the stock and bring up to the boil.
- Slice the rest of the washed potatoes thinly and add to the pot and simmer until these potatoes are tender and just cooked.
- Add the broad beans and double cream then season.
- Gently reboil and serve in four bowls with a tablespoon of crème fraîche on top of each along with some grated cheese.

New potatoes

Prawn cocktail

SERVES 4

SHOPPING LIST

350g shelled prawns
1 little gem lettuce
1 tbsp Dijon mustard
1 tbsp white wine vinegar
4 tbsp olive oil
Salt & freshly ground black pepper
6 tbsp mayonnaise
2 tbsp good tomato ketchup
1 tbsp double cream
1 tsp brandy
1 tsp creamed horseradish
Juice of ½ lemon
4 drops Tabasco sauce
2 tbsp finely chopped cucumber
1 avocado, diced
2 tomatoes, seeded and finely diced
1 shallot, peeled and finely chopped
1 tbsp chopped fresh chives

HOW TO CREATE THE DISH

- Put the prawns into a bowl.
- Finely shred the lettuce.
- Make a vinaigrette with the Dijon mustard, white wine vinegar and olive oil. Season with salt and pepper.
- Make the sauce by mixing the mayonnaise with the tomato ketchup and double cream, then stir in the brandy, horseradish, lemon juice and Tabasco. Check the seasoning.
- Mix the prawns with 1 tbsp of the sauce and 1 tbsp of the vinaigrette.
- Mix the shredded lettuce with the cucumber and diced avocado, add the remaining vinaigrette and season.
- Put the lettuce into four glasses, with the prawns on top. Cover lightly with the rest of the sauce.
- Mix the tomatoes, shallot and chives, sprinkle over the sauce and serve.

Prawns

Pressed smoked chicken with piccalilli

SERVES 20-24

SHOPPING LIST

3 whole smoked chickens
2 cloves garlic, chopped
8 whole carrots, peeled
1 onion, sliced
2 bay leaves
Parsley stalks
2 litres chicken stock
Small bunch tarragon
8 leaves gelatine
50g chopped capers
50g chopped gherkins
2tbsp chopped parsley
Salt & pepper
Piccalilli, to serve

HOW TO CREATE THE DISH

- Remove the skin from the chickens and reserve.
- Take the breasts off and keep whole.
- Take the rest of the meat off the bones and put to one side.
- Put the skin, bones, garlic, 2 carrots, onion, bay leaves and parsley stalks into a pan with the chicken stock and gently simmer for 30 minutes.

- Strain off and cook the remaining 6 carrots in the stock with the tarragon, take out the carrots and cool.
- Strain off 650ml of stock.
- Soften the gelatine in cold water, then dissolve in the stock.
- Line two terrine moulds with clingffilm with enough to overlap and cover the top of the terrines.
- Cut each breast into four strips lengthwise and put in a bowl.
- Chop the rest of the meat and mix with the chopped capers, chopped gherkins and chopped parsley, put in a bowl and season.
- Add 2tbsp of gelatine stock to each bowl and mix well.
- Lay strips of chicken breast on the bottom of the mould, then spread a layer of the chopped meat mixture on top, lay the whole carrots on top then chicken breast, then chopped meats.
- Continue until the terrine mould is well filled.
- Add more stock, then fold the cling film over and press the terrine with a weighted terrine mould on top.
- Refrigerate and press overnight.
- To serve, slice and add a garnish of piccalilli.

Gherkins

Risotto of mushroom and peas

SERVES 4

SHOPPING LIST

200ml vegetable stock

30g dried ceps

100g butter

1tbsp olive oil

1 finely chopped shallot

1 clove garlic, finely chopped

200g button mushrooms, sliced

150g Arborio rice

2tbsp double cream

100g frozen peas

Salt & pepper

30g grated parmesan cheese

30g shaved parmesan

HOW TO CREATE THE DISH

- Bring the stock up to the boil and add the dried ceps, take off the heat and leave to soak for 30 minutes.
- Melt 50g butter, add the olive oil and heat.
- Add the shallot and garlic, and sweat.
- Drain the ceps, keep the stock then chop the ceps and add to the shallot pan.
- Add the button mushrooms and fry for 2 minutes, then add the rice and stir till coated with oil and butter.
- Reboil the vegetable stock and add a ladleful at a time to the rice.
- Stir and leave to evaporate before adding the next ladleful.
- When the rice is cooked and the stock all absorbed, add the cream then the peas and season.
- Take from the heat, add the remaining butter and the grated parmesan cheese. Allow to stand for 5 minutes.
- Pour into bowls and serve with shaved parmesan on top.

Arborio rice

Roast chicken, pea and potato soup

I keep the carcasses of roast chicken, chopped and then frozen. They make a great saving however, if you haven't got anywhere to store these then start the soup by using 900g of chicken wings.

SERVES **4**

SHOPPING LIST

4 carcasses of roasted chicken
(plus all the jelly left when
roasting)
450g chicken wings
50g pork dripping
2 carrots, chopped
1 onion, choppped
1 clove garlic, chopped
4 tomatoes, chopped
1 sprig sage
1.8 litres water or chicken or
vegetable stock
Salt & pepper
350g potatoes
50g butter
225g frozen peas
2 tbsp parsley, chopped

HOW TO CREATE THE DISH

- Put the chopped carcasses, chicken wings and dripping into a roasting tray into a hot oven at 180°C and colour for 20 minutes.
- Add the vegetables and sage and roast for a further 30 minutes until well caramelised, but not burnt.
- Take out and put into a large pot with the water, chicken or vegetable stock.
- Bring to the boil, skim and simmer for 30 minutes. Strain and put back into a clean pan.
- Reduce to 1 litre in volume, then season.
- Peel and wash the potatoes and cut into 3mm thick slices then approximately 6 x 6mm.

- Melt the butter and add the potatoes.
- Slowly cook for approximately 10 minutes, do not colour or overcook.
- Add the stock, bring to the boil and simmer.
- Add the peas and season.
- Add the parsley and serve.

PS

- If you have some freshly roasted chicken breasts these can be diced and added at the serving time.

BRIAN TURNER

Butlins, Bognor Regis

Leisure pool

Brian Turner directs

Butlins

Summer is a fun-filled visit to Butlins – Britain's original holiday park. Celebrating over 75 years of success Butlins epitomises the ultimate British summer holiday. All the dishes on the Butlins menu are designed not only with flavour in mind but for that ultimate holiday feeling of pushing the boat out and trying something new.

The lambs liver is the perfect example of a 'new' dish, although it was a bit of a calculated gamble when I added it to the menu at the Turner's restaurant. It has excelled itself in popularity and I have even been told it was the best liver a customer had eaten! But don't worry if it's not your thing, the Turner burger is equally as delicious.

Restaurant opening

Restaurant

Roast chilli butternut squash and tomato soup

SERVES 6

1 medium butternut squash

1tbsp olive oil

2 cloves garlic, crushed

1 small green chilli, chopped

6 tomatoes, cut in half

1.8 litres chicken stock

Salt & pepper

2tbsp coriander, chopped

HOW TO CREATE THE DISH

- Peel and deseed the squash, chop into large pieces and put into a bowl.
- Add the olive oil, garlic and chilli and mix well.
- Put into the oven at 180°C in a tray and roast to caramelise some of the squash.
- After 10 minutes add the tomatoes.
- Take out and blitz in a food processor.

- Put into a large pan with the stock and bring to the boil.
- Season and simmer for 10 minutes.
- Pass through a sieve, check the seasoning, add the coriander and serve.

Butternut squash

Roasted pepper and tomato soup

SERVES **4**

450g red peppers
900g tomatoes
1 clove garlic
1tbsp oil
50g butter
110g onions, chopped
25g plain flour
1.8 litres chicken stock or vegetable stock
Salt & pepper

HOW TO CREATE THE DISH

- Cut the peppers in half, take out the seeds and stalks and put on a baking sheet.
- Cut the tomatoes in half and put on the sheet.
- Grate garlic over and add a splash of oil.
- Put in the oven at 230°C until just starting to colour.
- Melt the butter in a pan, add the onions and sweat, add the flour and cook for 3 minutes. Add the peppers and tomatoes and then the stock and season.
- Bring up to the boil and simmer for 45 minutes, skim off if necessary.
- Liquidise and put back into a clean pan.
- Reboil, season again and serve.

PS

- We use more, peeled roasted peppers as a garnish.

Red pepper

Smoked chicken, bacon and ginger soup

SERVES 10

SHOPPING LIST

12 smoked chicken thighs

3 litres smoked chicken stock

75g barley

175g onions, chopped into 6mm dice

110g celery, chopped into 6mm dice

175g leeks, chopped into 6mm dice

175g carrots, chopped

175g potatoes, diced

25g butter

2.5cm fresh ginger, finely grated

12 rashers back bacon

6 tomatoes, peeled, deseeded and chopped

3 tbsp chives, chopped

Salt & pepper

HOW TO CREATE THE DISH

- Put the chicken thighs into a pan with the stock and bring up to the boil.
- Skim off any scum and allow to simmer.
- Slowly cook for 15 minutes.
- Wash the barley and scatter into the stock.
- After 15 more minutes take out the thighs and leave to cool.
- Cook the barley for a further 45 minutes.
- Put the onions, celery, leeks and carrots into the stock.
- Cook for 15 minutes and then add the potatoes.
- When the vegetables and barley are cooked, dice the chicken flesh and put into the soup.
- Meanwhile, melt the butter and add the ginger, sweat but do not colour.
- Dice the bacon, add to the ginger and cook through.
- Add to the soup with the tomatoes and chives, check the seasoning and serve.

Ginger

Smoked salmon cushion with lemon vegetable salad

SERVES 4

SHOPPING LIST

4 large slices smoked salmon

100g fresh cooked salmon

2 tbsp mayonnaise

2 finely chopped shallots

2 tbsp chopped chives

1 tbsp lemon vinaigrette

50g diced cooked carrots

50g diced cooked swede

50g cooked peas

50g celeriac, cooked and diced

Salt & pepper

1 tbsp tomato concasse

Juice of 1 lemon

1 tbsp olive oil

Cress leaves

HOW TO CREATE THE DISH

- Lay each slice of smoked salmon on cling film.
- Flake the salmon into a bowl, but do not break it up too much.
- Add the mayonnaise, shallots, chives, vinaigrette, diced vegetables and peas, season and add juice of ½ lemon and allow to stand for 10 minutes.
- Spoon a quarter of the mix onto the centre of the smoked salmon.
- Pull in the sides of the smoked salmon then use cling film to pull in and seal gently into a ball shape.
- Push into a 5cm ring, joins uppermost, then put into a fridge to chill.
- Mix the tomato, juice of ½ lemon and olive oil, and season to make the dressing.
- Carefully take out the salmon, unwrap and turn over onto a plate.
- Put dressing around the salmon, decorate with the cress, brush the salmon with oil and serve.

PS

- We buy our salmon from Severn & Wye, it's the best.

Smoked salmon

Sweetcorn and brown shrimp cream soup

SERVES 4

SHOPPING LIST

4 large corn on the cob

50g unsalted butter

1 large onion, peeled and diced

1 clove garlic, peeled and chopped

1 stick celery, peeled and diced

1.5 litres vegetable or chicken stock

3 white peppercorns

2 sprigs fresh thyme

1 bay leaf

Salt & pepper

150ml whipping cream

150g brown shrimps, cooked

Squeeze lemon juice

Paprika, as required

HOW TO CREATE THE DISH

- Cut the kernels from the cobs.
- Cut each cob into three pieces through its diameter.
- Melt 25g butter in a thick-bottomed saucepan, add the onion, garlic and celery and cook without colour until everything softens.
- Add the cut corn cobs and stock along with the peppercorns, thyme and bay leaf.
- Bring to the boil and simmer for 30 minutes, strain and put to one side.
- Melt the remaining butter in a pan.
- Add the corn kernels, then add enough stock to cover and season.
- Simmer for 30 minutes until the corn is soft to the touch.
- Empty the contents of the pan into a food processor (or hand blender) and process until smooth.
- Pass through a fine mesh strainer, return to the pan and add the cream.
- Place the shrimps into individual soup bowls or a tureen and squeeze over some fresh lemon juice.
- Heat the soup and with a hand blender blitz the soup.
- Pour into the bowls or tureen, garnish with a fine dusting of paprika and serve.

Sweetcorn

Sweetcorn and spring onion soup

SERVES 4

SHOPPING LIST

100g unsalted butter

450g sweetcorn kernels cut from the cob

350g spring onions, shredded

25g sugar

1.2 litres chicken or vegetable stock

175g frozen sweetcorn kernels

300ml double cream

Salt & pepper

HOW TO CREATE THE DISH

- Melt 50g butter and add the fresh sweetcorn and half of the spring onions.
- Sweat, but do not colour, for 5 minutes.
- Add the sugar and stock, bring to the boil and simmer for 15 minutes.
- Take off and blend to a purée.
- Melt the remaining 50g butter, add the frozen sweetcorn with the rest of the spring onions and sweat for 5 minutes.
- Add the cream, bring to the boil and allow to simmer for 5 minutes.
- Add the purée and bring back to the boil, season and serve.

PS

- The combination of fresh and frozen sweetcorn can really be changed to any combination you want. All frozen goes well but some fresh makes the soup taste even better. This is a very simple soup to make but loved by all, especially young children.

Spring onions

Vegetable and herb soup

SERVES 4

HOW TO CREATE THE DISH

- Melt the butter in a pan.
- Add the shallots, leek, celeriac, garlic and carrots and sweat, but do not colour.
- Add the stock and bring to the boil, then simmer for 20 minutes.
- Add the courgettes, peas and cabbage and cook for 3 more minutes.
- Season and add the herbs and tomatoes
- Serve adding a splash of olive oil to each bowl.

PS

- This is almost like a green minestrone but fresher – it makes a great summer soup. I like to use chicken stock but have used vegetable stock here, the choice is yours. Please don't worry if you can't get all the herbs.

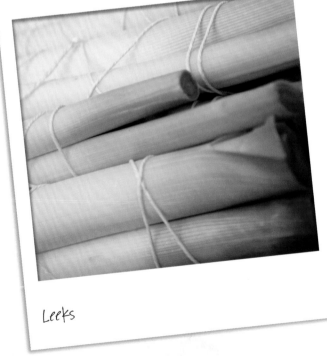

Leeks

Vichyssoise with a chopped soft-boiled egg and chives

SERVES 8

SHOPPING LIST

225g white of leek

50g butter

1.2 litres chicken or vegetable stock

450g potatoes, peeled and thinly sliced

150ml double cream

Salt & pepper

4 eggs

2 tbsp chives, chopped

HOW TO CREATE THE DISH

- Wash the leeks well in slightly warm water then shred finely.
- Melt the butter in a pan, add the leeks and sweat gently for 5 minutes, but do not colour.
- Add the stock and then the potatoes.
- Bring up to the boil and simmer for approximately 20 minutes.
- Skim.
- Liquidise then pass through a fine sieve into a clean pan.
- Add the cream, season and bring back to the boil.
- Soft boil the eggs for 6 minutes then plunge into cold water for 2 minutes.
- Take off the shell and chop, then scoop into soup bowls.
- Pour the soup over, sprinkle with the chives and serve.

PS

- Vichyssoise is a classic soup and as such should not be changed too much. The addition of the egg makes this a more substantial soup and so can be a snack meal with buttered bread.

Fresh eggs

Fish

Many people love fish but are not quite sure what to do with it when they get home. My advice would be to talk to your fishmonger and always look out for bright red eyes and fresh gills. Practice definitely makes perfect with fish and scallops are a great choice. Although they're not cheap to buy they really are a treat with a beautiful sweet flavour – always buy fresh and ask your fishmonger to remove the shells. The scallop and succotash recipe in this section is a perfect pairing as the sweet juicy succotash brings out the sweetness in the scallops. Or simply does it – enjoy scallops pan-fried, with crusty bread and lashings of good English butter.

Baked salmon fillet on a warm potato salad

SERVES 4

SHOPPING LIST

4 x 180g hot smoked salmon
pieces

100ml fish stock

100ml chicken stock

500g new potatoes, peeled

1tsp Dijon mustard

4tbsp mayonnaise

Juice of ½ lemon

4 spring onions, finely chopped

1tbsp chopped chives

Salt & pepper

HOW TO CREATE THE DISH

- Lay the salmon pieces in an oven-proof dish skin side up.
- Heat the fish stock and chicken stock together then pour round the fish. Heat in the oven to 180°C till the fish is hot, approximately 10 minutes, but do not allow to dry out too much.

- Meanwhile, cook the whole new peeled potatoes in boiling water until cooked.
- Take out, drain and slice into a bowl.
- Add 4tsp of hot stock from the fish and allow to stand for 20 minutes.
- Drain and put back into the bowl.
- Add the mustard, mayonnaise and lemon juice.
- Then add the spring onions and chives, and mix very carefully. Season.
- Put the potato salad on the plates.
- Lay a salmon piece on top of each, skin side up, and serve.

Lemons sliced in half

Brill fillet in morel and mushroom sauce

SERVES 4

SHOPPING LIST

50g butter

4 x 175g brill fillets

Salt & pepper

1 shallot, finely chopped

110g fresh morels, washed and cut in half lengthwise

110g button mushrooms, sliced

55ml dry sherry

150ml chicken stock

150ml double cream

50g cold butter

2 tbsp chopped chives

175g young spinach

25g butter

A little grated nutmeg

HOW TO CREATE THE DISH

- Melt 50g butter in a pan.
- Put the fish presentation side down in the hot butter and season.
- Colour lightly and turn over, then turn down the heat and cook for approximately 4-5 minutes, but do not overcook, baste frequently during cooking.

- Take out and keep warm.
- Add the shallot to the pan, then add the morels and button mushrooms.
- Sweat but do not over colour, then add the dry sherry and reduce to a syrup.
- Add the chicken stock and reduce by two-thirds, then add the cream.
- Boil until thickening then take from the heat and add the cold butter.
- Add the chives and season.
- Meanwhile wash the spinach.
- Melt 25g butter, add the spinach, season with salt and pepper and add a little grated nutmeg.
- Take out and drain.
- Put a little spinach in the middle of each plate.
- Lay the fish on top.
- Pour the sauce over and serve.

PS

- If fresh morels are not available use dried morels – soak for 2 hours in a little water and treat as fresh when cooking. Use the water which has had the morels in it, strained into the sauce.

Morel mushrooms

Deep-fried mussels and tomato tartare

SERVES 4

SHOPPING LIST

1.2 litres large mussels
2 shallots, chopped
140ml dry white wine
4tbsp tomato passata
110g seasoned flour
2 eggs, beaten
350g brioche crumbs or
breadcrumbs
300ml mayonnaise
25g capers, chopped
50g gherkins, chopped
1tbsp chopped parsley
1tbsp chopped tarragon
Oil to deep fry

HOW TO CREATE THE DISH

- Clean and rinse the mussels and put into a heavy-based pan.
- Add the shallots and wine, cover and bring to the boil.
- Allow all the mussels to open then take out, drain and allow to cool.
- Carefully strain the juice twice, put into a pan with the tomato passata and reduce over a medium heat, take off and cool.
- Meanwhile pick (remove from the shells) the mussels and dry.
- Coat them individually in seasoned flour, then the beaten eggs and then the breadcrumbs.
- Roll them individually between your hands to make sure the mussels are well coated and the crumbs do not fall off easily.

- Meanwhile mix the reduced tomatoes with the mayonnaise, capers, gherkins, parsley and tarragon.
- Deep fry the mussels, take out and drain, dry and serve with the tomato tartare.

Mussels

Grilled lemon sole with marrowfat peas

SERVES 4

SHOPPING LIST

200g marrowfat peas
1 tablet bicarbonate of soda
4 x 400g fresh lemon sole
120g butter
Salt & pepper
50g butter
Juice of 1 large lemon

HOW TO CREATE THE DISH

- The night before, put the peas into a pot with lots of water and the bicarbonate of soda tablet.
- Trim the sole of the head, dark skin and angel wings.
- Wash and dry well.
- Grease a tray with 50g butter.
- Lay the fish on top and smear with the remaining 150g butter.
- Put under a grill until cooked through, take out, baste with butter and season.
- Rinse the peas then put them into a pot with plenty of water.
- Bring up to the boil and simmer till cooked.
- Drain, heat with 50g butter and season.
- Serve the fish with the peas and squeeze lemon juice over.

Lemon sole

A Taste of Summer with Brian Turner

FISH
FISH

Grilled loin of tuna, crushed potato and caramelised fennel cake, roasted pepper salsa

Fennel

Grilled loin of tuna, crushed potato and caramelised fennel cake, roasted pepper salsa

SERVES 4

SHOPPING LIST

POTATO CAKE:
260g baking potatoes
80g butter
10ml olive oil
1 bulb fennel, finely chopped
1 tbsp fennel fronds, chopped
Salt & pepper
50g plain flour

RED PEPPER SALSA:
1 large red pepper
30ml olive oil
6-8 large ripe tomatoes
4 cloves garlic, peeled and finely chopped
Juice of 1 lime
½ bunch fresh coriander
Salt & pepper
2 green chillis
1 medium onion, peeled and finely chopped

TUNA:
4 x 180g tuna steaks
Salt & pepper
50ml olive oil
1 lime

HOW TO CREATE THE DISH

Potato cake:

- Bake the potatoes in their skins and scoop out the cooked flesh.
- In a pan heat 40g butter with a little olive oil.
- Add the finely chopped fennel, season and cook until the fennel is soft and nicely caramelised.
- Add the fennel to the potatoes along with the chopped fennel fronds and mix, season to taste.
- Divide the mix into four equal-sized portions, shape into 2.5cm thick circles and dust in a little flour.
- Pan fry each side in the remaining butter until a nice golden crust is formed on both sides.
- Keep warm until required.

Red pepper salsa:

- Rub the pepper with oil, place into a hot oven at 200°C and roast until blackened, approximately 15 minutes.
- Remove from the oven and cover, ensuring that the steam doesn't escape.
- Once cool enough to handle remove the skin and the seeds, then cut into ½ cm dice.
- Cut the tomatoes into quarters and remove the seeds, then cut the remaining flesh into 5mm dice.
- Mix the peppers and tomatoes together, add the garlic, lime juice, chilli and onion, and finally add the chopped coriander.
- Stir well and season liberally.
- Place in the fridge for at least 2 hours before serving.
- Take out and add oil, then serve.

Tuna:

- Heat a frying pan or ribbed grilling pan to a very high temperature.
- Season the tuna steaks and rub well with the olive oil.
- Place into the pan and cook for approximately 30 seconds – 1 minute each side, depending on how thick the steaks are.
- Just before the tuna is removed from the pan squeeze over fresh lime juice.

To serve:

- Place a potato cake onto the plate and top with the tuna steak. Serve a little salsa over and the rest separately.

Punting

Summer is punting on meandering rivers and letting nature take its course

Grilled pickled mackerel fillet on a celeriac and apple salad

SERVES 4

SHOPPING LIST

2 x medium mackerel
Salt & pepper
2 shallots
6 peppercorns
1 sprig thyme
1 bay leaf
Peel of ½ lemon
300ml white wine vinegar
150ml white wine
175g celeriac
1 green apple
1tsp mustard
2tbsp cider vinegar
8tbsp olive oil
1tbsp shredded parsley
Olive oil

HOW TO CREATE THE DISH

- Fillet and trim the mackerel, take out the pin bones, sprinkle lightly with salt and put to one side.
- Shred the shallots and add to the peppercorns, thyme and bay leaf in a saucepan.
- Add strips of lemon peel, vinegar and the wine.
- Bring to the boil and simmer for 5 minutes.
- Lay the mackerel fillets in a tray and strain the hot liquor over.
- Leave to cool for 20 minutes.
- Take out and drain.
- Meanwhile slice the celeriac thinly and cut into strips, blanch in boiling salted water for 1 minute, take out, drain and cool.
- Cut the apple into slices then into strips.
- Mix three-quarters of the apple with the celeriac.
- Mix together the mustard, vinegar and 8tbsp olive oil then add half the parsley and season.
- Mix a quarter of this with the celeriac and apple and check the seasoning.
- Cut the remaining apple into small dice and mix with the remaining dressing, then add the rest of the parsley.
- Put the mackerel onto a tray and sprinkle with olive oil.
- Gently grill under a hot grill until cooked.
- Put some salad in the middle of the plates. Lay the mackerel on top, pour the dressing around and serve.

Mackerel

A Taste of Summer with Brian Turner

Herb-crusted tuna salad, poached quails' eggs, sweet pepper and caper aioli

Jar of peeled red peppers

Herb-crusted tuna salad, poached quails' eggs, sweet pepper and caper aioli

SERVES 4

HOW TO CREATE THE DISH

Herb crust:
* Blend the bread and herbs together in a food processor.
* Add the butter in small amounts until a paste is formed.
* Put to one side.

Poached quails' eggs:
* Place a medium pan of water on to boil.
* Once at a rolling boil, add the vinegar and salt.
* Using a serrated knife cut off the bottom of the shell and drop the egg into the water.
* Poach for 2 minutes, remove from the water and place straight into a bowl of iced water – this will set the egg.

Pepper and caper aioli:
* Drain the red peppers.
* Place all the ingredients, except the capers, in a food processor and blend until smooth.
* Remove into a bowl, add the capers and adjust the seasoning.
* Store in the fridge until ready to use.

Tuna:
* Using some oil grease the base of a grill pan/roasting dish.
* Season the tuna and sear each side then smear one side with a thin film of Dijon mustard.
* Place some of the herb crust onto the mustard-smeared tuna steak, pack it tightly and make sure there is an even coverage.
* Place under a moderate grill or in the oven at 220°C for no longer than 4-5 minutes.

To serve:
* Mix the baby leaves and dress with the olive oil and balsamic vinegar and season.
* Place onto a plate.
* Top with the herb-crusted tuna, drizzle with some of the aioli and garnish with quails' eggs.

SHOPPING LIST

2 shallots
1 sprig thyme
6 peppercorns
1 bay leaf
Peel of ½ lemon
300ml white wine vinegar
150ml white wine
Salt & pepper
4 x 110g seat trout fillets
(boneless and skinless)
50g pea purée
1tsp Dijon mustard
2 egg yolks
Juice of ½ lemon
½ pt rapeseed/groundnut oil
Salt & cayenne pepper
1tbsp olive oil
4 spring onions
½ tsp Dijon mustard
1tbsp white wine vinegar
4tsp light olive oil
1tbsp chopped chives
Pea shoots

Lightly pickled west coast sea trout with pea mayonnaise, pea shoots and spring onion dressing

SERVES 4

HOW TO CREATE THE DISH

- Shred the shallots, then add to a pan with the thyme, peppercorns, bay leaf, lemon peel, vinegar, wine and salt.
- Bring up to the boil and simmer for 5 minutes.
- Pour over the sea trout and leave to cool a bit – make sure they are cooked but not too much (keep warm).
- Make the mayonnaise by adding the pea purée to 1tsp Dijon mustard and the egg yolks.
- Add the lemon juice, beat in the oil and season with salt and cayenne pepper.
- Make the dressing by first heating the oil.
- Shred the spring onions and add to the oil.

- Soften quickly and take off the heat.
- Put into a bowl, add the ½ tsp Dijon mustard and vinegar and mix together.
- Stir in the olive oil and season.
- Add the chives.
- Serve by putting a dollop of mayonnaise in the centre of the plate and swirl it around. Lay the warm fish on top. Pour some dressing over and around and decorate with the pea shoots.

Roasted skate wings on butterbean stew with spicy sausage

SERVES 4

SHOPPING LIST

225g dried butter beans
4 x 225g skate wings
1tsp black pepper from a mill
1tsp paprika
110g butter
Salt
2tbsp white wine vinegar
150ml chicken stock
110g hot chorizo sausage
1tsp olive oil
½ onion, finely chopped
1tbsp chopped parsley

HOW TO CREATE THE DISH

- Bring the butter beans up to the boil in a pan full of water.
- Simmer until tender, approximately 1 hour.
- Take off the heat, drain and keep to one side.
- Trim the skate wings and dry off.
- Mix the pepper with the paprika and sprinkle on one side of each of the skate pieces.
- Melt the butter and colour the peppered side of the skate gently for 2 minutes then turn over and season with salt and put in the oven at 180°C for approximately 10 minutes or until cooked, then take out and drain.
- Pour off half of the fat from the roasting tray and add the vinegar, swill around to soak up the juices then add the stock.
- Strain into a clean pan, bring to the boil and reduce.
- Meanwhile cut the sausage into 6mm dice.
- Heat the oil, add the sausage and colour, cook then add the onion, sweat and add the beans, stock, parsley and season with salt.
- Spoon the beans into a bowl and lay the skate on top to serve.

Chorizo sausage

Seaside

A Taste of Summer with Brian Turner

Summer is building crumbling sandcastles and paddling on the sea shore

SHOPPING LIST

SAFFRON-ROASTED SALMON:
4 x 180g salmon fillets
¼ tsp saffron strands
½ clove garlic, finely chopped
1tsp capers, finely chopped
1dsp finely chopped fennel green tops
Salt & pepper
50ml olive oil

WARM CANNELLINI BEAN SALAD:
10ml extra virgin olive oil
½ clove garlic, crushed
1tsp snipped sage leaves
Salt & pepper
1 x 300g tin whole cannellini beans, drained
½ cucumber, peeled, seeded and cut into fine dice
Fresh lemon juice, to taste

ROASTED VINE TOMATOES:
400g red cherry tomatoes on the vine
Olive oil
Salt & pepper

OLIVE OIL, ORANGE AND BASIL SAUCE:
6tbsp olive oil
Finely grated zest of 2 oranges
2 cloves garlic, finely chopped
Juice from 1 orange
20 kalamata pitted olives
Salt & freshly ground black pepper
30g fresh basil leaves, chopped

Saffron-roasted salmon, warm cannellini bean salad, roasted vine tomatoes, olive oil, orange and basil sauce

SERVES 4

HOW TO CREATE THE DISH

Saffron-roasted salmon:
* Mix all the ingredients apart from the salmon together.
* Marinate the salmon overnight in the mixture.
* Place onto a roasting tray and roast in an oven at 180°C for 15 minutes.

Warm cannellini bean salad:
* Heat the oil gently with the garlic, add the sage along with the lemon juice and infuse, season and add the drained beans and cucumber, keep warm.

Roasted vine tomatoes:
* Drizzle the tomatoes with the olive oil and seasoning.
* Roast in a low oven at 140°C until they just start to collapse.
* Keep warm.

Olive oil, orange and basil sauce:
* Warm the olive oil in a medium pan.
* Add the orange zest and garlic, then cook for 1 minute.
* Add the orange juice and olives and season.
* Add the basil and reserve.

To serve:
* Put the beans in a bowl with the tomatoes, place the salmon fillet on top and dress with the sauce.

Tomatoes

Seared scallops on a bed of succotash

SERVES 4

SHOPPING LIST

175g dried butterbeans
150ml oil
2 rashers back bacon
1 onion, finely chopped
1 red pepper, diced
2 sweetcorn cobs
150ml chicken stock
2tbsp double cream
2tbsp chopped parsley
12 scallops
50g curry powder
Salt & pepper

HOW TO CREATE THE DISH

- To make the succotash bring the butterbeans up to the boil in lots of unsalted water for approximately 1 hour.
- Drain and take off the heat.
- Put a splash of oil into a pan.
- Chop the bacon into thin strips, add to the pan and colour.
- Turn down the heat, add the onion and pepper, and sweat.
- Cut the kernels from the cobs, add to the onion mixture and stir well.
- Add the stock and bring to the boil.
- Add the beans and season.
- Reduce the stock and add the cream, bring to the boil till it thickens and then add the parsley.
- Dip one side of the scallops gently into the curry powder then sear quickly in hot oil.
- Turn over, season and cook gently.
- When cooked, take out and drain.
- Scoop the succotash into bowls.
- Lay three scallops per person on top and serve.

Scallops

Tower of fresh and smoked salmon, tomato, dill and lemon dressing

SERVES 4

TOMATO, DILL AND LEMON DRESSING:

3 sticks lemongrass

100ml vegetable stock

1dsp coriander seeds

1 lemon, washed, seeds removed and blitzed to a purée in a food processor until completely smooth

100ml olive oil

3 tomatoes, cut into quarters and seeds removed

1 small bunch of dill, finely chopped

Salt & pepper

SALMON AND SMOKED SALMON TOWER:

800g very fresh salmon fillet, skin and bone removed

300g sliced smoked salmon

Salt & pepper

100ml olive oil

Lemon juice

HOW TO CREATE THE DISH

Tomato, dill and lemon dressing:

- Smash and chop the lemongrass and add to the vegetable stock.
- Crush the coriander seeds and add to the stock.
- Bring to the boil, reduce by half and then remove from the heat, add the lemon purée and allow to cool and infuse for a couple of hours or for best results overnight.
- Strain, add the oil and mix thoroughly.
- Cut the tomatoes into a fine dice, add the dill and the lemon dressing.
- Season to taste.

Salmon and smoked salmon tower:

- Using a 9cm round cutter cut the salmon into four neat pieces, then cut each piece in half horizontally.
- Gently rub with olive oil, season lightly and place into the oven at 60°C and leave for 10 minutes.

- On a board cut out 12 circles from the smoked salmon the same size as the fresh salmon, then sprinkle with a little lemon juice and black pepper.
- Build the tower with 1 piece of smoked salmon, then 1 piece of the fresh salmon, then 1 smoked salmon, 1 fresh and then topped neatly with the last piece of smoked salmon.
- Repeat this for all four portions.

To serve:

- Centre the salmon on each plate. Pour the tomato, dill and lemon dressing over.

Tuna with 'salsa verde'

SERVES 4

SHOPPING LIST

4 × 175g tuna loin steaks

2tbsp olive oil

Salt & pepper

1 bunch flat leaf parsley

1 small chilli

1 clove garlic, crushed

10 midget gherkins

1tbsp capers

2tbsp white wine vinegar

4tbsp extra virgin olive oil

HOW TO CREATE THE DISH

- Brush both sides of the tuna steaks with oil then grill on a charcoal-type grill.
- Mark criss-cross style on one side then turn over and finish cooking and season.
- To make the salsa verde finely chop the parsley, chilli, garlic, gherkins and capers together.
- Add the vinegar then the olive oil and season with pepper from a mill.
- Put the tuna on a plate, spoon the salsa verde over and serve.

Garlic

Meat

Meat

Although summer signifies hazy days and warm nights, we all know that the British weather can be somewhat unpredictable. So for those days when summer is less than summery, the chicken faggot dish in this section is the perfect light but warm dish. They're a classic for me and signify my traditional upbringing (I used to eat them on the way to school!) Although they can be tricky a little bit of practice goes a long way, and even if you don't fancy faggots then chicken is a lovely summer meat. My best advice is to learn how to carve, that way you can make the most of the chicken meat and then freeze the bones for stocks or sauces later.

Beef olives with turned root vegetables

SERVES `4`

SHOPPING LIST

BEEF OLIVES:

4 x 175g slices of topside beef

25g unsalted butter

50g breadcrumbs

½tsp chopped thyme

1tsp chopped parsley

1tbsp chopped cooked bacon

1 egg

Salt & pepper

50g dripping

1 onion, finely chopped

1 carrot, finely chopped

1 clove garlic

1tbsp tomato purée

140ml red wine

850ml brown beef stock

TURNED ROOT VEGETABLES:

12 pieces turned (evenly shaped) carrot

12 pieces turned swede

12 pieces turned potatoes

12 button onions

110g butter

Salt & pepper

1tbsp chopped parsley

HOW TO CREATE THE DISH

Beef olives:

- Tap the slices of topside out evenly between two layers of plastic.
- Melt the butter, add the breadcrumbs, herbs and bacon then the egg and season, mix together.
- Smear equal parts onto each tapped-out piece of meat (removed from the plastic), season and roll up.
- Tie with thin string to hold everything together.
- Heat the dripping, seal and colour the olives in the hot fat then take out.
- Add the chopped vegetables and colour lightly.
- Add the garlic and then the tomato purée.
- Stir and add the red wine, then reduce.
- Lay the olives in the pan and add the brown stock.
- Bring to the boil, cover with greaseproof paper and a lid, put into the oven at 170°C and cook for 1-1½ hours.
- When cooked take out the olives then leave to rest.
- Reduce the sauce, pass through a sieve, check the seasoning and consistency.
- Remove the string carefully from the olives, pour the sauce over and reheat.

Turned root vegetables:

- Cook the vegetables separately in boiling salted water.
- Refresh in cold water.
- Drain.
- Reheat slowly in the butter, then season.
- Serve with the meat.

Carrots

Braised beef stew with tomatoes and spring onions

SERVES 4

HOW TO CREATE THE DISH

- Heat the oil in a large pan.
- Add the beef in batches and fry to a good colour.
- Take out and keep to one side.
- Add the onion and garlic to the oil to start to colour.
- Add the tomato purée and stir, then add the wine and reduce by two-thirds.
- Put the beef back in and add the stock, carrots, celery and tinned tomatoes.
- Add the herbs and bring up to the boil.
- Simmer with a lid on for approximately 1¼ hours until just cooked.
- Carefully take out just the meat and keep warm.
- Pass the sauce through a liquidiser and then a strainer.
- Return to the pan and add the meat, finish cooking.
- Add the concasse tomatoes and three-quarters of the spring onions.
- Cook for a further minute then serve sprinkled with parsley, the rest of the spring onions and mashed potatoes.

Red wine

Cauliflower cheese cottage pie

SERVES **4**

HOW TO CREATE THE DISH

- Heat the oil in a pan, add the beef and fry to colour.
- Add the onion and garlic and fry.
- Add 25g flour and mix in well.
- Add the tomatoes, Worcestershire sauce and 150ml stock.
- Leave to cook slowly for 30-45 minutes.
- Add more stock if necessary.
- Meanwhile cook the potatoes, swede and carrots in water, drain, dry and pass through a ricer.
- Add seasoning and 50g butter.
- Pour the meat into an ovenproof dish and allow to cool.
- Lay the mashed potatoes mix on top of the meat and smooth.
- Meanwhile cook the cauliflower in water.
- At the same time boil the milk with the ½ onion. Also melt 25g butter, add 25g flour and stir in the milk/onion mixture.
- Beat smooth and take from the heat, add half the cheese and the egg yolk, then season.
- Drain the cauliflower and carefully place the florets on top of the potato.
- Pour the sauce over and sprinkle with the rest of the cheese.
- Bake in the oven at 200°C for 30 minutes until well coloured.

Cauliflower

Chicken faggots

SERVES 4

HOW TO CREATE THE DISH

- Mince the chicken liver, thigh meat and belly pork together.
- Put into a pan with the garlic and onion and stew slowly for 20 minutes, lid on, but do not colour.
- Strain off the fat then put the mixture into a bowl.
- Add the herbs and nutmeg and season, then add the egg.
- Add enough breadcrumbs to make an easy-to-handle mixture.
- Divide into approximately 50g balls and wrap in as little caul as possible to hold together.
- Put into an ovenproof dish touching each other.
- Pour the stock over, enough to come halfway up the faggots.
- Bake in the oven at 180°C for 45 minutes until brown on top.

Breadcrumbs

Chicken lasagne

SERVES 6-8

SHOPPING LIST

450g dried lasagne sheets

1 large onion

2 carrots

1 stick celery

4 rashers back bacon

4 tbsp olive oil

2 cloves garlic, crushed

450g minced chicken

2 x 285g tins plum tomatoes, chopped

140ml dry white wine

150ml brown stock

Salt & pepper

75g butter

75g flour

850ml milk

2 tbsp double cream

2 egg yolks

110g grated Fontina cheese

225g cooked spinach

HOW TO CREATE THE DISH

- Plunge the lasagne sheets into boiling salted water and cook for 10 minutes.
- Take out and put into cold water to refresh.
- Chop the onion finely with the carrots and celery.
- Dice the bacon finely.
- Heat the olive oil in a pan and put the vegetables and bacon into the oil with the garlic.
- Fry until soft but do not colour.

- Add the chicken and cook for about 5 minutes.
- Add the tomatoes, wine, stock and season.
- Cover and gently cook for about 45 minutes.
- Meanwhile melt the butter, add the flour and cook, but do not colour.
- Slowly add the milk and bring to the boil each time, beating out the lumps.
- Take off the heat and add the cream.
- Split in half and put the egg yolks and half the cheese into one half.
- Put the spinach in the other half and season both.
- Drain the lasagne sheets.
- Put a little cheese sauce on the bottom of the dish.
- Lay lasagne sheets on top, put half the chicken sauce on top and lay lasagne sheets on top.
- Spread the spinach sauce on this and then lay lasagne sheets on top.
- Put the rest of the chicken sauce on top and then a layer of lasagne sheets.
- Spread with the remaining cheese sauce, sprinkle with the rest of the cheese and bake in the oven at 200°C for 20 minutes.

Sheets of pasta

Corned beef hash cakes on tomato chutney

SERVES 4

HOW TO CREATE THE DISH

- Mix the mashed potatoes with the corned beef.
- Season with a splash of Worcestershire sauce, salt and pepper.
- Mould into even-shaped balls.
- Coat with the flour, then the beaten egg, then the breadcrumbs.
- Fry in melted dripping and colour on all sides.

- Meanwhile chop the onion and cook in the butter.
- Add the tomatoes, cut into pieces, and cook slowly for 10 minutes with the sugar, vinegar, salt and pepper.
- Add the parsley at the last minute.
- Put the tomato chutney on the plates.
- Lay the hash cakes on top and serve.

PS

- The corned beef hash cakes can be deep or shallow fried.

Single serving

Tennis

Summer is the rediscovered joy of tennis on plush grass courts

A Taste of Summer with Brian Turner

Corn-fed chicken, French-style peas, potato wafer and chicken gravy

Peas

SHOPPING LIST

CHICKEN:
4 corn-fed chicken breasts, skin on with wing bone still attached
50ml olive oil
50g butter

POTATO WAFER:
3 large old potatoes
50g melted butter
Salt

FRENCH-STYLE PEAS:
50g butter
100g button onions, peeled and blanched
Salt & pepper
285ml chicken stock
500g frozen peas, blanched for 30 seconds in boiling water, removed and cooled rapidly in cold water
1 small lettuce, shredded
5g plain flour

CHICKEN GRAVY:
300g chicken wings
50g butter
1 onion, finely chopped
½ leek, finely chopped
1 stick celery
2 cloves garlic, peeled and chopped
⅛ bunch thyme
1 bay leaf
600ml chicken stock

Corn-fed chicken, French-style peas, potato wafer and chicken gravy

SERVES 4

HOW TO CREATE THE DISH

Chicken:

- Carefully remove the meat surrounding the chicken wing bone to leave an exposed, clean bone.
- Heat the oil in a large frying pan, melt the butter into the oil then, keeping at a medium heat, fry the chicken for 3 minutes either side.
- Place back onto a lightly buttered tray and into the oven at 200°C for a further 10 minutes, until golden brown and cooked through.
- Put to one side and keep warm.

Potato wafer:

- Peel the potatoes and, using a mandoline, slice them as evenly and thinly as possible. Place into cold water so they don't discolour.
- Brush some of the melted butter onto a baking tray, dry the potato slices and lay out one by one, slightly overlapping.
- Brush the tops with a little more butter and season.
- Put some parchment paper on top of the potatoes and place a baking tray on top of this so that the potatoes are compressed.

- Place into the oven at 200°C and cook for approximately 10-15 minutes.
- When cooked the wafers should be golden and very crisp.
- Cut to shape and put to one side.

French-style peas:
- Melt 40g butter in a pan and add the onions, season and coat in the butter for 1 minute.
- Cover with the chicken stock and cook for 5 minutes.
- Add the peas, lettuce and remaining butter.
- Cook for 30 seconds, sprinkle in the flour and cook for another 30 seconds.
- Adjust the seasoning and put to one side.

Chicken gravy:
- In a thick-bottomed pan colour the chicken wings in 25g butter, add the chopped vegetables and herbs.
- Add the stock.
- Bring to the boil and skim well.
- Cook for 30 minutes approximately.
- Pass through a sieve, return to the pan and reduce by half.
- Shake in the remaining butter.

To serve:
- Put the peas on the plates, lay a chicken breast over, garnish with the potato wafer and pour the gravy around.

Ginger and tomato lamb cutlets

SERVES 4

SHOPPING LIST

2 cloves garlic

2tbsp grated ginger

3tbsp groundnut oil

8 tomatoes, deseeded and quartered

8 lamb cutlets

½ red onion, finely chopped

1 pinch chilli powder

½tsp turmeric

425ml chicken stock

Salt

16 new potatoes, cooked

½ red onion, finely sliced

1 spring onion, finely shredded

HOW TO CREATE THE DISH

- Crush the garlic and ginger together.
- Heat 2tbsp oil, add the garlic and ginger and fry lightly, then add the tomatoes and cook together.
- In a separate pan heat 1tbsp oil and colour the lamb cutlets.
- Take out and put into the tomato mix.
- Add the onion, chilli powder and turmeric and heat in the pan.
- Add the stock and season.
- Pour over the lamb, bring to the boil, put on a lid and cook in the oven at 180°C for 45 minutes.
- Take out, take the lid off and add the potatoes.
- Put on the heat and reduce the liquor by one-third.
- Serve in the dish, sprinkle with the onion and spring onion, and serve.

Ginger

Grilled chicken breast with summer vegetable salad

SERVES 4

SHOPPING LIST

200g frozen peas

125ml chicken stock

8 pieces asparagus

8 button mushrooms

8 button onions

50g cherry tomatoes

50g butter

Salt & pepper

1tbsp chopped parsley

4 x 200g chicken breasts

1tbsp virgin olive oil

New potatoes, to serve

HOW TO CREATE THE DISH

- Cook 100g of peas in the stock and blend.
- Add 100g peas then cooked asparagus, cooked button mushrooms, onions and cherry tomatoes.
- Add butter and shake in, then season and add chopped parsley.
- Meanwhile take off the chicken skin, trim the bone and tap out the breast nice and thin.
- Rub with olive oil and cook on a chargrill on both sides, then season.
- Using a slotted spoon, put the vegetables on a plate.
- Lay a chicken breast on top, pour the sauce over and serve with new potatoes.

Button mushrooms

Grilled pork bangers with fried potatoes and onion

SERVES 4

SHOPPING LIST

2 tbsp sunflower oil

8 premium pork sausages

100g unsalted butter

2 large onions, thinly sliced

200ml thickened chicken stock

600g new potatoes cooked in skins

Salt & pepper

2 tbsp chopped parsley

HOW TO CREATE THE DISH

- Heat a medium frying pan and add 1tbsp sunflower oil.
- Colour the sausages evenly, cook for 10 minutes.
- Finish by cooking on grill bars or alternatively cook in a grill pan for 20-25 minutes.
- Put to one side.
- Meanwhile melt 25g butter and add the sliced onions, colour lightly then slowly cook for 10 minutes, add 2tbsp chicken stock and cook till the stock evaporates and the onions are coloured well.
- Melt 25g butter, slice the new potatoes, add to the butter and colour.
- When coloured, mix the onions and potatoes together, and season.
- Pile the potatoes in the middle of the plates and carefully arrange the sausages around.
- Boil the sauce left in the pan and add 50g cold butter.
- Pour the sauce around the sausages, sprinkle with parsley and serve.

Sliced onion

Lamb pencil fillets, mustard and balsamic

SERVES 4

SHOPPING LIST

1tbsp olive oil

8 lamb pencil fillets

12 new potatoes, cooked in their skins

1tbsp pommery mustard

16 cherry tomatoes

Salt & pepper

1tsp balsamic vinegar

150ml chicken stock

50g cold butter

1tsp chopped parsley

HOW TO CREATE THE DISH

- Heat the oil in a large frying pan.
- Colour the lamb fillets then take them out.
- Cut the potatoes in half lengthwise and put the cut side into the pan.
- Brush the lamb fillets with mustard and then lay on the potatoes.
- Cut the tomatoes in half and add to the pan, season then put in the oven at 200°C for 8 minutes.
- Take the meat out, then the potatoes and allow them to rest.
- Discard any excess oil, add the balsamic and reduce, then take out the tomatoes.
- Add the stock, butter and parsley and bring to the boil.
- Put the tomatoes and potatoes on the plates.
- Arrange the lamb on top.
- Pour the sauce over and serve.

PS

- Pencil fillets are the ones from under the saddle of the lamb and are rarely used.

New potatoes

Mustard crust cottage pie

SERVES 4

HOW TO CREATE THE DISH

- Heat the oil in a pan.
- Slice the onion, crush the garlic and add to the pan.
- Allow to soften and start to colour.
- Add the meat, colour and seal, breaking up any lumps.
- Take out of the pan and put to one side.
- Cut the swede and potatoes into 6mm dice and add to the pan.
- Colour slightly and add back in the meat.
- Add the Worcestershire sauce and grain mustard.
- Stir in well, add half the stock and bring to the boil, reduce the heat and simmer gently, stirring regularly.
- Add the stock as it dries out – keep it moist but not wet.
- When cooked, add tomatoes and season, and cook for a further 10 minutes. Put into serving dishes.
- Soften the butter and mix well with the Dijon mustard.
- Cut the bread into circles.
- Butter with the mustard mix.
- Lay carefully on top of the mince, butter side up.
- Put into an oven heated to 200°C.
- Cook for 10-20 minutes until the mustard colours.

Grain mustard

Croquet

A Taste of Summer with Brian Turner

Summer is the clack of hard wooden balls rolling sweetly through teasing hoops on uneven turf

Pan fried lambs' liver with capers and parsley sauce

SERVES 4

SHOPPING LIST

8 slices fresh lambs' liver
1tbsp groundnut oil
Salt & pepper
100g unsalted butter
100g midget capers
Juice of ½ lemon
2tbsp chopped parsley
16 cooked skinned new potatoes

HOW TO CREATE THE DISH

Midget capers

- Trim the liver and drain on a cloth.
- Heat the groundnut oil and quickly fry the liver on both sides, take out and season. Keep warm.
- Throw away the oil and add 50g butter
- Add the capers and as the butter starts to turn golden, add the lemon juice and parsley.
- Meanwhile slice the potatoes, colour lightly in 50g butter, then season.
- Put the potatoes on the plate and lay two slices of liver on top.
- Pour the caper sauce over and serve.

SHOPPING LIST

2 crowns of chicken
2tbsp curry powder
1tbsp groundnut oil
25g butter
1tbsp clarified butter
½ apple in small dice
150g mirepoix (carrot and onion), small dice
1tbsp curry powder
300ml chicken stock
150ml full-fat milk
150ml double cream
Juice of 1 lemon
1tbsp chopped parsley
Salt & pepper
½ red pepper
½ yellow pepper
1 courgette
2tbsp seasoned flour
4tbsp double cream
100g clarified butter
25g clarified butter
½ finely chopped onion
250g basmati rice
400g chicken stock
25g butter

Roast crown of chicken with Indian spices, red and yellow peppers and courgettes, basmati rice and curry essence

SERVES 4

HOW TO CREATE THE DISH

* Rub the crowns of chicken with 2tbsp curry powder.
* Heat the oil in a roasting pan, add the chicken and roast in the oven at 180°C for approximately 30 minutes.
* After 5 minutes add the butter and baste frequently.

Red and yellow peppers

* When cooked take out and rest upside down.
* Heat the 1tbsp clarified butter, add the apple and mirepoix and lightly colour.
* Add 1tbsp curry powder, stir in and add the stock and milk, and heat until cooked.
* Take off the heat, blend then strain into a clean pan.
* Add the cream, lemon juice and parsley, and season.
* Trim the peppers and cut into diamond shapes. Cut the courgette into slices.
* Dust with the seasoned flour, dip into the cream and fry in 100g clarified butter.
* Heat 25g clarified butter, add the onion and sweat, but do not colour, add the rice and stir round. Add the stock and stir, then bring up to the boil.
* Cover with greaseproof paper, put into the oven at 180°C and cook for 15 minutes.
* Take out, season and add the butter, then let it rest.
* To serve, put the rice in centre of the plate, the chicken on top, the vegetables around and pour the sauce over

PS

* Crown of guinea fowl makes a nice change.

Roast leg of English lamb with garlic heads served with roast marrow filled with a spicy bean casserole

SERVES 4

HOW TO CREATE THE DISH

- Pour boiling water over the heads of garlic.
- Trim off the tops and use these to rub over the prepared leg of lamb.
- Put the lamb into a roasting tray and season, splash with oil and put into the oven at 200°C for 1¼ – 1½ hours.

Roasted leg of lamb

- After 45 minutes season the remaining garlic heads with salt and pepper and put into the roasting tray, take out after 25 minutes and keep warm.
- Meanwhile cut the marrow in half lengthwise and scrape out the seeds.
- Brush with some butter, season and put into the oven at 180°C.
- At the same time, cook the beans separately in boiling salted water for approximately 10 minutes until cooked.
- Melt 50g butter, add the onion and sweat, but do not colour.
- Add the chilli, sweat then add the wine, reduce by half and add the tomatoes.
- Add the beans and heat together.
- After 40 minutes remove the marrow, fill with the beans, cover with breadcrumbs and return to the oven.
- Cook for a further 40 minutes, if too coloured cover with foil.
- Take out and leave to rest with the lamb.
- Serve the lamb sliced with a head of garlic and a slice of marrow.

SHOPPING LIST

- 700g piece centre cut fillet of beef (21 days hung)
- 50g dripping
- 1tsp chilli flakes
- 1tsp garlic salt
- 1tbsp chopped and dried parsley
- ¼ tsp curry powder
- Salt & pepper
- 1 cup flour
- 1 cup eggs
- 1 cup milk/water
- 1 pinch salt
- 1tbsp malt vinegar
- 12 pickled onions, medium sized
- 1tsp vegetable oil
- 25g butter
- 50g dripping (reserved from earlier)
- 450g swede
- 75g butter
- 1.2 litres chicken stock
- 25g butter
- 1 shallot, chopped
- 140ml white wine
- 70ml Madeira
- 150ml meat stock
- 150ml double cream
- ¼ tsp English mustard
- 1tbsp horseradish cream sauce
- 1tbsp chopped parsley

Roast spiced fillet of beef with roast pickled onion Yorkshire pudding, braised swede and English mustard and horseradish cream sauce

SERVES 4

HOW TO CREATE THE DISH

- Tie the fillet with string to keep its shape.
- Heat the dripping and seal the outside.
- Take off the heat and allow to cool – do not throw away the dripping.
- Put the chilli into a coffee grinder, then add the other spices and grind to a fine powder.
- Roll the beef in the spices to cover all sides, season with salt then roll in cling film and leave for 3 hours.
- Put into the oven in the tray used to seal the meat at 180°C for 10 minutes.
- Turn the oven down to 160°C, turn the meat over and cook to your required temperature/liking.
- Take out and keep warm.
- Meanwhile, for the Yorkshire puddings, make the batter by mixing together the flour, eggs, milk/water, pinch of salt and malt vinegar, then pour into very hot small muffin trays with the dripping preheated and bake in the oven at 210°C for approximately 25 minutes.
- At the same time, colour the onions in the oil, add the butter, season and cook in the oven at 210°C for 10 minutes.
- When cooked take both out and keep warm.
- Shape the swede into one large piece per person.
- Colour one side in 50g melted butter.
- Turn over, season, add the chicken stock and bake in the oven at 180°C, brush with more melted butter during cooking.
- Take out and keep warm.
- Make the sauce by melting 25g butter, add the shallots, sweat but do not colour.
- Add the wine and reduce by two-thirds, add the Madeira and reduce by one-third.
- Add the meat stock and reduce by half.
- Add the cream and boil till starting to thicken.
- Take off the heat, add the mustard and horseradish and strain into a clean pan.
- Check the seasoning, then add the parsley.
- Carve the beef into four steaks and put in the middle of the plates.
- Put the onions into the Yorkshire puddings and place round the beef.
- Put the swede on the plates and swirl sauce around the plate, serve some separately.

PS

- The Yorkshire pudding ingredients are in cups because it's the volume of the mix and not the weight. You can use a tea cup or a mug but ensure you use the same vehicle each time.

Turner's own burger steak

SERVES 4

SHOPPING LIST

720g coarsely minced beef
1 finely chopped shallot
1 clove garlic, crushed
1tbsp chopped parsley
1tsp Dijon mustard
1 big splash Worcestershire sauce
1tbsp double cream
2tbsp chopped midget gherkins
Salt & pepper
2tbsp groundnut oil
Chips, buns, salad, to serve

HOW TO CREATE THE DISH

- Chill the meat well.
- Add all the ingredients, season and leave to marinate for at least 2 hours.
- Wet your hands and shape into four even-sized burger steaks.
- Brush the steaks with oil and cook on a hot, oiled chargrill till nice and brown; finish if necessary in an oven.
- Serve with chips, bun and salad garnish.

PS

- Because our burger is so popular with young children at Butlins we cook the patties slightly longer than we would normally do.

Minced beef

Barbecues

Barbecues really typify summer for me, that chargrilled smell, meat off the bone or skewer and that happy if not a little bit overpowering smokey smell that comes with the barbecue territory. Barbecue food really is the easiest food to make – just soaking your chicken or beef in a marinade and then adding to a hot grill can make a fantastically quick dish. The Kofta kebabs in this section are so quick and easy – they go down fantastically well with a fresh salad and a glass of wine. If you're using wood skewers make sure you soak them first, and when serving to guests push a fresh skewer alongside to replace the charred one that way they're fresh and easy to remove.

Brian cooking on the bbq

Barbecue kindly supplied by Weber.
For more information visit www.weber.com

Barbecue cutlets on a tomato relish salad

SERVES 4

HOW TO CREATE THE DISH

Barbecue cutlets:

- Trim the rack of lamb.
- Cut into double cutlets and clean the bones.
- Mix the almonds, onion and garlic in a food processor.
- Deseed and chop the chillies, peel and chop the ginger and add to the almond mixture.
- Add the yoghurt and make a paste.
- Add the spices and salt then pour into a bowl.
- Dip the lamb into the marinade and leave overnight.
- Take out and brush off excess marinade.
- Brush with oil and grill for 6 minutes or until cooked.
- Take off and rest, serve with the tomato relish salad.

Tomato relish salad:

- Mix the mustard with the vinegar, then add the oil, salt and pepper.
- In another bowl, mix the tomatoes, onion, coriander, chilli, pepper and cumin.
- Dress the salad leaves by pouring relish over.

To serve:

- Lay the chops on top of the salad standing up and sprinkle with more relish dressing.

Red chillies

Barbecued sardines

SERVES 4

SHOPPING LIST

12 large fresh sardines

12 sprigs fresh lemon thyme

3 tbsp olive oil

2 cloves garlic, crushed

1 tsp finely grated lemon zest

1 tbsp lemon juice

Splash of Tabasco

Salt & pepper

2 lemons

HOW TO CREATE THE DISH

- Have the fish carefully scaled and gutted.
- Dry and stuff each cavity with the lemon thyme.
- Mix the oil, garlic, lemon zest and juice, and Tabasco.
- Marinate the fish in the mixture for 3 hours.
- Take out and cook on the barbecue, use excess marinade to baste the fish, season when cooked.
- Serve with half a barbecued lemon on each plate.

Lemons

Chargrilled asparagus

SERVES 4

SHOPPING LIST

24 pieces of green and white
asparagus
2tbsp oil, to cook
Salt
3tbsp olive oil
1tbsp balsamic vinegar
110g shaved parmesan cheese
Black pepper from a mill

HOW TO CREATE THE DISH

- Trim the asparagus of the wooden ends and cut to the same length.
- Plunge into boiling salted water for 30 seconds and then into iced water to refresh.
- Dry off and put onto a tray with 2tbsp oil and season with a little salt.
- Cook on the barbecue till tender, approximately 3-4 minutes.
- Take off and put on a dish.
- Mix the 3 tbsp olive oil and vinegar together, and pour over the asparagus.
- Sprinkle the cheese over the asparagus and top with lots of freshly ground black pepper.

Parmesan

Kofta Kebab

SERVES 4

SHOPPING LIST

50ml vegetable oil

3 cloves garlic, minced

1 large onion, peeled and finely diced

2 green chillis, deseeded and finely chopped

1tsp ground coriander

1tsp ground cumin

800g minced lean lamb

1 bunch coriander, finely chopped

Salt & pepper, to taste

½ bunch fresh mint, finely chopped

60g fresh breadcrumbs

8 x 15cm wooden skewers soaked in warm water

Salad and flatbread, to serve

Minted yoghurt, optional, to serve

HOW TO CREATE THE DISH

- Heat a frying pan with the oil, add the garlic, then the onion, then the chilli, coriander and cumin and soften with no colour.
- Remove from the heat and cool.
- In a large bowl add the remaining ingredients along with the cooled onion mixture.
- Using your hands, work the mixture until amalgamated.
- If the mix is too wet, add more breadcrumbs until you have a firm but malleable mixture.
- Divide the mix into 8 equal portions and squeeze the meat onto the skewers in a sausage shape.
- Place in the fridge to rest for at least 1 hour.
- Barbecue until cooked all the way through, approximately 10-12 minutes.
- Serve with salad and flatbread and garnish if required with minted yoghurt.

Coriander

Lemon and thyme chicken kebabs

SERVES 6

HOW TO CREATE THE DISH

- In a bowl mix the lemon juice, zest, thyme, salt and pepper, mustard and ketchup.
- Add the chicken and coat completely, cover and allow to marinate for at least 2 hours.
- Thread onto the skewers until the skewer is fully loaded.
- Preheat a barbecue until the heat is even and hot.
- Place the chicken on the barbecue and cook, turning every minute for about 15 minutes, depending on the thickness of the chicken.
- The chicken centre needs to be above 75°C (test with a meat thermometer) for it to be cooked thoroughly.
- Serve on the skewer with salad and flatbread.

Thyme

Noisettes of lamb with an asparagus, radish and pear dressing

SERVES 4

1 loin of lamb

2 garlic cloves, crushed

1tbsp chopped parsley

Salt & pepper

Oil, for frying

1tsp mustard

4tbsp white wine

2tbsp olive oil

1tbsp chopped parsley

8 cooked asparagus spears

1 pear

6 radishes

HOW TO CREATE THE DISH

- Trim the loin of lamb and trim off the excess flap of fat, tap out.
- Mix garlic and parsley and a pinch of salt.
- Lay on the meat, pull the fat over, trim and tie.
- Cut into eight equal pieces.
- Brush with oil and barbecue the noisettes of lamb.
- Keep pink, take off and keep warm.
- Meanwhile mix the mustard with the wine, then add the oil and parsley, and season.
- Take 4cm of tips off the asparagus and reserve. Cut the stems into small slices.
- Cut the pear and radishes into the same size and mix with the asparagus.
- Add the dressing and check the seasoning.
- Put the noisettes on a plate.
- Pour the dressing over and around.
- Put the asparagus tips on top and serve.

Radishes

BRIAN TURNER

A Taste of Summer with Brian Turner

Summer is the sounds
of laughter and the
giddy excitement of a
summer fair

Paprika chicken legs on roast tomatoes

SERVES 4

SHOPPING LIST

1 tbsp olive oil
Juice of ½ lemon
1 tbsp paprika pepper
4 good size chicken legs
6 tomatoes. cut in half
1 clove garlic, chopped
2 tbsp oregano
1 tbsp olive oil

HOW TO CREATE THE DISH

- Mix the tablespoon of oil, lemon juice and paprika and add the chicken.
- Mix well and leave for 2-3 hours.
- Heat a roasting tray and colour the skin side of the chicken legs on top of the stove.
- Turn over and place in the oven to roast at 200°C for about 20 minutes.
- Meanwhile put the tomatoes into another roasting tray cut side up and sprinkle with garlic, a little oregano and tablespoon of oil.
- Roast for 10 minutes.
- Take out the legs and put onto the barbecue skin side down.
- Continue to cook, turning over regularly.
- Put the tomatoes on the barbecue to finish.
- Take off and put three halves of tomatoes on a plate.
- Lay a chicken leg on top and sprinkle with the oregano.

Paprika

Spiced chicken koftas with sesame seed and parsley dressing

SERVES 3

SHOPPING LIST

450g chicken flesh from legs and breast

¼ tsp chilli flakes

1tsp coriander seeds

½ tsp mustard seeds

2 cloves garlic

1tbsp chopped parsley

Salt & pepper

1tbsp olive oil

3 soaked wooden skewers

2tsp sesame seeds, toasted

1tbsp chopped parsley

1 clove garlic, crushed

½ tsp finely grated lemon zest

½ tsp sesame seed oil

3tbsp olive oil

1tbsp lemon juice

Salt & pepper

HOW TO CREATE THE DISH

- Mince the chicken into a bowl.
- In a spice blender mix the next four ingredients nice and fine.
- Add to the chicken and mix well.
- Allow to stand for 1 hour.
- Add the tablespoon of parsley, salt and pepper.
- Test fry a small amount of the mix in a little olive oil – taste and check for seasoning.
- Oil your hands and make into even-sized sausage shapes around the soaked wooden skewer.
- Cook on a barbecue for approximately 10 minutes until nicely coloured and cooked inside.
- Meanwhile mix the sesame seeds with the parsley, garlic and lemon zest.
- Add the sesame seed oil, 3 tablespoons olive oil and lemon juice, and season.
- Serve with the koftas.

Sesame seed oil

Sticky BBQ spare ribs

SERVES 4

1.3kg pork spare ribs

1 chicken stock cube

1 onion

1 carrot

1 leek

1 tsp black peppercorns

8 tbsp hoisin sauce

1½ tbsp clear honey

3 cloves garlic, crushed

2 tbsp dry sherry

1 tbsp cider wine vinegar

1 tbsp soy sauce

1 tsp five-spice powder

HOW TO CREATE THE DISH

The day before:

- Cut the sheets of ribs into three- or four-ribs sections.
- Put a pan of water on to boil and add the stock cube and cleaned vegetables.
- Put the ribs in and boil for 30 minutes.
- Meanwhile put the peppercorns into a hot dry wok until they start to smell.
- Take out and grind to a powder.
- Put into a bowl with the rest of the ingredients and mix.
- Mix the ribs in the marinade and stir well.
- Leave overnight.

On the day:

- Barbecue slowly for about 15 minutes and serve.

Honey

Stuffed pork fillet in bacon

SERVES 4

SHOPPING LIST

4 x 150g pork fillets, centre cut
4 tbsp chutney
2 tbsp chopped pine kernels
4 bacon rashers
2 tbsp olive oil
2 tbsp lime juice
1 clove garlic, crushed
1 tsp chopped oregano
Salt & pepper

HOW TO CREATE THE DISH

- Cut a pocket in the middle of each pork fillet.
- Mix the chutney and pine kernels together and stuff into the pork.
- Wrap the bacon tightly round each fillet to keep the chutney mixture in.
- Fix with a soaked cocktail stick.
- Mix the oil with the lime juice, garlic and oregano.
- Marinate the pork in the oil mixture for 2 hours and season with salt and pepper.
- Take out and barbecue, turning regularly and basting with the oil mixture, till cooked.

Chutney

Tuna steaks on courgettes with chermoula

SERVES 4

HOW TO CREATE THE DISH

- To make the chermoula heat a dry pan and add the cumin, paprika, garlic and cayenne and dry fry for 30 seconds.
- Pour out into a cold bowl and add the parsley, coriander, lemon juice and 2 tbsp olive oil.
- Mix 2tbsp of olive oil and 1tsp of cumin together.
- Thinly slice the courgettes horizontally then put into the oil/cumin mix and season.
- Dip the tuna steaks into the oil/cumin mix and grill quickly on the barbecue, keeping them pink in the middle.
- Meanwhile quickly grill the courgettes on the barbecue, when cooked put onto a dish.
- Place the tuna on top and drizzle the chermoula over.

Courgettes

Desserts

Desserts

Summer is the best time for desserts, there is just no doubt about it – fresh berries, cream, ice cream – anything works well on a midsummer evening. Fruit desserts are a number one choice for me as they can be fresh but are also warming for days when the sun goes back to bed. The blueberry and apple bread and butter pudding is definitely my dessert choice as my dad used to make it, plus you can eat it hot or cold, with ice cream, cream or custard and the tanginess of the blueberries really burst out. For something lighter sorbet or fruit is another summer must-have dessert – so simple but delicious.

Apple meringue crumble with coffee custard

SERVES 4

HOW TO CREATE THE DISH

- Peel, core and cut the apples into 6mm dice.
- Melt the butter and add the apples, sugar and Calvados and cook slowly until starting to 'fall' apart.
- Take from the heat and cool. When cold crumble in the meringue shells.
- Meanwhile rub the butter into the oats and flour to a sandy texture then mix with the sugar and hazelnuts. Spread on a baking tray and bake at 180°C for 15 minutes, take out and cool.
- At the same time, put the cream, coffee and vanilla pod on to boil.

- Cream the sugar and egg yolks, add the cream mixture and put back on the heat. Slowly cook to thicken.
- Take off, strain and cool.
- Put the apple mixture into glasses and sprinkle with the crumble.
- Cover with the cold custard and leave to set, then serve.

SHOPPING LIST

275g Bramley apples
50g unsalted butter
25g caster sugar
2tbsp Calvados
175g meringue shells
110g unsalted butter
110g toasted pinhead oats
110g plain flour
75g unrefined caster sugar
50g toasted chopped hazelnuts
300ml double cream
4tbsp strong coffee
1 vanilla pod
110g unrefined caster sugar
6 egg yolks

Coffee beans

Banana and toffee pudding

SERVES 6

HOW TO CREATE THE DISH

- Melt the 50g butter with the 50g sugar.
- Add the golden syrup and bring up to the boil.
- Add the cream, reboil and cook for 2-3 minutes.
- Add the chopped peanuts and remove from the heat.
- Cream the butter and 110g sugar and add the beaten eggs slowly.
- Mash the bananas and mix in.
- Sift the flour and baking powder and add to the mix, but do not overmix.
- Put the toffee sauce into six greased moulds/ramekins.
- Put half of the pudding mixture on top.
- Share out the rest of the toffee sauce.
- Fill up with the rest of the pudding mix.
- Bake at 170°C for 25 minutes.
- Take out and leave to rest for 5 minutes.
- Turn out carefully, sprinkle with icing sugar and serve.

PS

- Serve with glazed banana and clotted cream.

Bananas

Blueberry and apple bread and butter pudding

SERVES 4–6

HOW TO CREATE THE DISH

- Cut the muffins into 1¼ cm dice.
- Heat the 300ml cream with the vanilla pod.
- Mix the caster sugar with the eggs and egg yolk.
- Pour the cream onto the sugar mix and whisk.
- Take out the vanilla pod.
- Cut the apples into 6mm dice, toss in 25g butter then add to the cake mix with the blueberries.
- Pour the custard over.
- Divide into buttered dariole moulds.
- Bake in the oven at 160°C for 30 minutes until set.

- To make the sauce, melt the butter, brown sugar and golden syrup together till golden brown.
- Take from the heat and add the 150ml cream.
- Allow to reboil, take off the heat and allow to cool slightly.
- Turn out the puddings and put into bowls.
- Serve the sauce around.

Blueberries

Coconut rice pudding with Nigel's jam

SERVES `4`

HOW TO CREATE THE DISH

- Wash the rice and drain.
- Bring the cream and coconut milk to the boil.
- Shower in the rice and stir.
- Add the sugar, split vanilla pod and butter.
- Simmer slowly, stirring regularly until cooked, approximately 45 minutes.
- Heat the jam carefully.
- Pour the pudding into dishes, lay the jam in the centre and serve.

PS
- Nigel is our head chef at Butlins Bognor Regis and is a great man for the seasons and foraging; so his homemade jam (probably made by Susan, his wife) is fab and changes regularly!

Fresh jam

Cranachan

SERVES 4

SHOPPING LIST

75g pinhead oats

225g raspberries

600ml double cream

4tbsp runny honey

4tbsp malt whisky 'Glenfarclas'

HOW TO CREATE THE DISH

- Toast the oats in the oven until golden or in a dry frying pan, then cool.
- Blitz 50g raspberries in a food processor to make a purée.
- Whip the cream.

- Stir in the honey and whisky, and mix well.
- Carefully stir in the raspberry purée and three-quarters of the oatmeal.
- Spoon into martini glasses, sprinkle the rest of the raspberries and oatmeal over, and serve.

Raspberries

Harvest

Summer is harvest gold
punctuated with hay
bales scattered from
horizon to horizon

Iced passion fruit with gingered lychees

SERVES 4-6

1 egg
2 egg yolks
100g caster sugar
80ml passion fruit pulp
300ml whipped double cream
Squeeze lemon juice
275g tinned lychees
50g crystallised ginger in syrup

HOW TO CREATE THE DISH

- Place a pan of water on the heat to boil.
- Put the egg and egg yolks with the caster sugar into a mixing bowl that will sit over the saucepan of hot water.
- Whisk gently until light and fluffy and double in volume – do not allow to get too hot.
- Take off the heat and fold in the passion fruit pulp.
- Beat in one-third of the cream then fold in the remaining cream.
- Add the lemon juice.
- Pour into a clingfilm-lined 500ml loaf tin, cover with cling film and freeze for at least for 6 hours.
- Meanwhile, drain the lychees.

- Chop the ginger into fine dice.
- Mix together and allow to infuse for 2 hours.
- Take the iced passion fruit from the freezer and remove the cling film.
- Slice with a hot knife and put on a plate.
- Pour the lychees and ginger on top, and serve.

PS
- I serve with drizzle of raspberry coulis.

Passion fruit

Mango and coconut pancakes

SERVES 4

HOW TO CREATE THE DISH

- Mix the first seven ingredients to make the batter and leave to rest.
- Heat the oil in a pan 15cm diameter
- Fry the pancakes, flip over, take out and keep warm in a clean tea towel.
- Peel the mango and cut into fine dice.
- Take half the clotted cream and mix with the mango.

- To serve, put a pancake on the plate, then a spoon of mango and cream on top.
- Repeat, then finish with a pancake.
- Put a blob of clotted cream on top, sprinkle with toasted coconut and serve.

Coconut

Marmalade bread and butter pudding

SERVES 4–6

SHOPPING LIST

1 loaf brioche bread
100g unsalted butter
6tbsp marmalade
300ml milk
300ml double cream
1 vanilla pod
2 whole eggs
6 egg yolks
125g caster sugar
8 oranges, cut into segments

HOW TO CREATE THE DISH

- Slice the bread and butter one side of each slice.
- Lay into a buttered 1 litre pie dish, butter side up.
- Sprinkle the marmalade over, then put on a second layer of bread.
- Meanwhile, heat the milk and cream with the vanilla seeds scraped in.
- Mix the eggs, yolks and sugar together.
- Strain the milk mixture over the egg mixture then pour this over the bread in the pie dish.
- Allow to stand for 30 minutes.
- Cook in a tray with water half-way up the pie dish in the oven at 160°C for 30-40 minutes.
- Take out of the oven and serve with the oranges.

PS

- To make a more sophisticated dish for dinner parties, allow to cool, cut into 6cm ring shapes and reheat.

Marmalade

Orange fool

SERVES 6

HOW TO CREATE THE DISH

- Sandwich two discs of sponge cake with the marmalade.
- Put orange segments into the bottom of the martini glasses.
- Put a sandwich of sponge on top.
- Mix the citrus rind and juices with the sugar thoroughly.
- Whip 425ml cream until thick but not stiff.
- Slowly beat the juices into the cream.
- Spoon over the cake and chill until the cream sets and the juice has separated over the cake, preferably overnight.
- Whip the rest of the cream and pipe on top, decorate as desired and serve.

Oranges

Raspberry and blackberry pavlova

SERVES 6

SHOPPING LIST

90g egg whites
Squeeze lemon juice
1 tbsp cornflour
90g caster sugar
425ml double cream
225g blackberries
225g raspberries
Icing sugar, as required
150ml raspberry coulis

HOW TO CREATE THE DISH

- Whisk the egg whites to soft peaks in a food processor.
- Mix the lemon juice and cornflour together then add half the sugar, add to the whites and whisk to soft peaks again.
- Add the rest of the sugar and beat for 5 more minutes to stiff peaks.
- Draw a 25cm circle onto non-stick parchment.
- Turn over and put on a tray, use to make the pavlova shape using a piping bag and plain tube.
- Bake at 140°C for 30 minutes, turn off the oven and leave for 1 hour to cool slowly.
- Whisk the cream to soft peaks, add the blackberries and pile into the middle of the meringue.
- Decorate with the raspberries, shake icing sugar over and serve with the raspberry coulis.

Blackberries

BRIAN TURNER

Golf

A Taste of Summer with Brian Turner

Summer is the ebb
and flow of fortune
as you drive and
putt your way
across the fairest
greens

Sesame apple turnovers with apricot sauce

SERVES 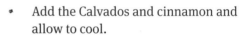 4

HOW TO CREATE THE DISH

- Roll out the pastry.
- Cut 10cm rounds and leave to rest, covered up.
- Peel and trim the apples and then cut into small dice.
- Add to the butter and sugar in a pan and cook slowly, but do not overcook.
- Add the Calvados and cinnamon and allow to cool.
- Brush the edges of the pastry with water.
- Put the apple filling in the centre of the pastry, fold over and seal.
- Brush with the egg white.
- Dip into the sugar then the sesame seeds.
- Put onto a baking sheet and bake at 220°C for 15 minutes.
- Meanwhile, melt the apricot jam and bring to the boil.
- Mix the cornflour and water and use to thicken the sauce.
- Pass through a fine sieve and serve with the turnovers.

Apples

Stuffed peaches

SERVES 8

HOW TO CREATE THE DISH

SHOPPING LIST

8 firm ripe peaches, halved and stoned

55g shelled walnuts

6 macaroons or 6 whole amaretti di Saronno

55g heavy cream

1 egg yolk

2 tbsp Cognac

1 tbsp caster sugar

Peaches

- Deepen the hollow in each peach half then place the peaches in a buttered 30cm baking dish, hollow side facing upwards.
- In a food processor, grind the walnuts and macaroons until crumbly. Combine with the cream, egg yolk, Cognac and sugar. Stuff each hollow with the mixture – any excess can be placed between the peach halves. Bake in the oven at 180°C for 20 minutes.
- Serve warm.

Trifle

SERVES 6

SHOPPING LIST

BASE:

1 Swiss roll

2 bananas

225g raspberries

VANILLA CUSTARD:

300ml full-fat milk

300ml double cream

1 vanilla pod, split

4 egg yolks

2 eggs

115g caster sugar

FINISHING:

1 sherry glass sweet sherry (or as much or as little as you like!)

115g raspberry jam

300ml double cream

25g caster sugar

55g chopped pistachios

HOW TO CREATE THE DISH

Base:

- Cut the Swiss roll into slices or chunks and lay in the bottom of a large glass bowl or individual glass bowls (it used to be the best crystal bowl!). Peel and slice the bananas, then sprinkle over the Swiss roll. Scatter the raspberries on top and leave to one side.

Vanilla custard:

- Put the milk and double cream on to boil in a medium pan with the scraped vanilla pod and seeds. Put the egg yolks, eggs and sugar into a bowl and beat well together. Pour the hot cream mixture on to the eggs and mix well.
- Put this mixture into a clean pan and heat gently, stirring carefully, to allow the custard to thicken slightly. Do not let it curdle. Pull off the heat, put into a cold container and leave to cool.

Finishing:

- When the custard is cool, pour the sweet sherry over the fruit and sponge in the bowl or bowls. Now pour the cooled custard over. Refrigerate and allow to set (overnight is good).

- Warm the jam then allow it to cool a little, but while still runny, pour it over the custard. Allow to set.
- Whip the cream with the sugar and put into a piping bag. Decorate the top of the trifle with this, then carefully sprinkle the pistachios over the cream.

PS

- Serve with glazed banana and clotted cream.

Pistachios

Warm lemon curd pudding

SERVES 6

SHOPPING LIST

175g butter

175g caster sugar

3 eggs, beaten

2 lemons juice and zest (grated)

175g self-raising flour

50ml full-fat milk

400g lemon curd

110g butter, for greasing

HOW TO CREATE THE DISH

- Lightly butter six ramekin dishes.
- Beat the butter and sugar until really light and pale.
- Add the eggs a little at a time, beating well between each addition until fully incorporated.
- Stir in the lemon juice and zest.
- Lightly stir in the flour.
- Adjust with the milk until you get a dropping consistency.
- Put the lemon curd in the bottom of the buttered ramekins and then fill up with the sponge mixture.
- Cover with buttered paper or aluminium foil.
- Put into a steamer and cook for approximately 1 hour.
- When cooked leave to stand for 10 minutes then turn out to serve.

Finishing touch

Cocktails

For the ultimate taste of summer it has to be Pimms. Fruity, refreshing and easy to drink a glass in hand is the signature sign of a great British summer. I serve mine with bags of fruit and mint and have enjoyed a glass at Henley, Ascot, Goodwood and regular local cricket matches and barbecues. It's fantastic because it's such a great talking point with everyone fishing out the odd stray strawberry from their glasses. Plus it can be jazzed up further in order to make a Turbo Pimms with an extra shot of vodka. And for the kids a fun and colourful fruit punch or zingy traditional lemonade is the perfect refreshment after all their running around.

Pimms

'This is a really fresh-tasting drink, the fruit really brings out the flavour of the Pimms – a perfect summer classic.'

NEED:

Highball tumbler	Straws
Ice	Strawberries, sliced
Cucumber, sliced skin and flesh	Orange, sliced
Lemon, sliced	Fresh mint
Pimms	Lemonade

METHOD:

- Fill the base of the tumbler with fruit, cucumber and mint and mix well together with the straw.
- Add ice up to the top of the glass and mix again.
- Add 2 parts of Pimms and then top up with lemonade.
- Mix together with the straw and garnish with cucumber skin and fresh mint.
- Serve.

Classic Martini

'This cocktail needs to be very cold to drink, this is a classic British recipe, the version with the olive is American and known as a dirty martini.'

NEED:

Martini glass	Shaker
Strainer	Ice
Extra-dry Martini	Tanqueray gin
Lemon zest	

METHOD:

* Add ice to a martini glass to chill and leave to one side.
* Fill a shaker with ice and add 1 part of martini.
* Shake well to coat the shaker and then discard the martini, keeping the ice.
* Add 2 parts of gin to the ice in the shaker and mix well.
* Discard the ice from the glass and fill with strained gin from the shaker.
* Zest the lemon over the glass so the natural oils from the lemon are added to the gin.
* Add a slice of zest and serve.

Long Island Iced Tea

'Invented in the USA in the 1930s prohibition period this 'iced tea' was aptly named because it smelt and looked like iced tea – yet had a few extra ingredients that made it more than just tea.'

NEED:

Shaker	Highball glass
Ice	Straw
Triple sec	White rum
Vodka	Gin
Tequila	Lemon juice
Cola	Lemon slice

METHOD:

* Fill a shaker with a shot of each of the spirits and mix well.
* Fill a tumbler with ice and pour over the spirit mix.
* Add a squeeze of lemon juice and top up with cola.
* Garnish with a lemon slice and a straw.

Pina Colada

'A totally tropical drink, this is perfect for getting in that holiday spirit or just relaxing in the garden – it can also be made child friendly with just the removal of the rum for a great-tasting summer drink.'

NEED:

Blender	Large wine glass
Straw	Ice
Coconut milk	White rum
Pineapple juice	Pineapple slice

METHOD:

- In a blender add the ice, 2 parts coconut milk, 3 parts rum and 5 parts pineapple juice.
- Blend until smooth and pour into a glass.
- Garnish with a slice of pineapple, add a straw and serve.

Tequila Sunrise

'From the depths of Mexico the Tequila Sunrise shows the fantastic colours of a stunning summer sunset, yellow to red.'

NEED:

Highball glass	Stirrer
Ice	Tequila
Orange juice	Grenadine
Orange slice	Orange zest

METHOD:

- Add ice to a glass.
- Over ice pour 1 part Tequila and top up with orange juice.
- Mix together with a stirrer.
- Slowly add the grenadine so that it sinks to the bottom.
- Decorate with a slice of orange and some orange zest.

Lemonade

'Great for kids and grown-ups this refreshing drink is a classic summer staple. You can amend the sugar or lemon content to your taste or add zest if you wish.'

NEED:

Ice	Large wine glass
1 tsp White sugar	Lemon juice
Water	Lemon, sliced

METHOD:

- Add ice to a glass.
- Mix all the ingredients together according to your taste.

Fruit Punch

'Perfect for thirsty mouths, this punch works well in a jug or bowl with a ladle at summer parties and barbecues.'

NEED:

Ice	Jug
½ Granny Smith apple	1 orange, diced
200ml Cranberry juice	200ml Pineapple juice
200ml Orange juice	Soda water

METHOD:

- Add ice to a jug, then add the apple and orange.
- Add all the juices into the jug and top up with soda water.
- Mix together and serve.

APPLE

Apple meringue crumble with coffee custard p200
Blueberry and apple bread and butter pudding p204
Grilled pickled mackerel fillet on a celeriac and apple salad p110
Roasted breast of quail on a Waldorf salad with a green apple dressing p28
Sesame apple turnovers with apricot sauce p224

APRICOT

Sesame apple turnovers with apricot sauce p224

ASPARAGUS

Asparagus, mustard and herb salad with a radish dressing p10
Chargrilled asparagus p178
Noisettes of lamb with an asparagus, radish and pear dressing p184
Pea, courgette, cucumber, spring onion and asparagus salad, on little gem leaf with a radish dressing p26

ARTICHOKE

Jerusalem artichoke and mussel cream soup p62

AVOCADO

Avocado and coconut soup p46
Salad of breast of chicken with avocado, cherry tomatoes and herb dressing p30

BACON

Smoked chicken, bacon and ginger soup p82
Stuffed pork fillet in bacon p194

BALSAMIC

Lamb pencil fillets, mustard and balsamic p156

BANANA

Banana and toffee pudding p202

BARBECUE

Barbecue cutlets on a tomato relish salad p174
Barbecued sardines p176
Chargrilled asparagus p178
Kofta kebab p180

Lemon and thyme chicken kebabs p190
Noisettes of lamb with an asparagus, radish and pear dressing p184
Paprika chicken legs on roast tomatoes p188
Spiced chicken koftas with sesame seed and parsley dressing p190
Sticky BBQ spare ribs p192
Stuffed pork fillet in bacon p194
Tuna steaks on courgettes with chermoula p196

BEAN

Roasted skate wings on butterbean stew with spicy sausage p118
Roast leg of English lamb with garlic heads served with roast marrow filled with a spicy bean casserole p166
Saffron-roasted salmon, warm cannellini bean salad, roasted vine tomatoes, olive oil, orange and basil sauce p122
Scallop and bean salad with a raisin dressing p36

BEEF

Beef olives with turned root vegetables p132
Braised beef stew with tomatoes and spring onions p134
Corned beef hash cakes on tomato chutney p142
Roast spiced fillet of beef with roast pickled onion Yorkshire pudding, braised swede and English mustard and horseradish cream sauce p168
Turner's own burger steak p170

BEETROOT

Roast baby beet, potato and blue cheese salad p40

BLACKBERRY

Raspberry and blackberry pavlova p220

BLUEBERRY

Blueberry and apple bread and butter pudding p204

BREAD

Blueberry and apple bread and butter pudding p204
Marmalade bread and butter pudding p216

BRILL

Brill fillet in morel and mushroom sauce p98

BUTTERNUT SQIASH

Roast chilli butternut squash and tomato soup p78

CAPER

Herb-crusted tuna salad, poached quails' eggs, sweet pepper and caper aioli p112
Pan fried lambs' liver with capers and parsley sauce p162

CASSEROLE

Roast leg of English lamb with garlic heads served with roast marrow filled with a spicy bean casserole p166

CAULIFLOWER

Cauliflower cheese cottage pie p136

CARROT

Carrot salad with mint, orange and garlic dressing p12

CELERIAC

Celeriac remoulade p14
Grilled pickled mackerel fillet on a celeriac and apple salad p110

CELERY

Celery and Wensleydale cream soup p48

CHEESE

Cauliflower cheese cottage pie p136
Celery and Wensleydale cream soup p48
Macaroni cheese with slow-cooked cherry tomatoes p64
Roast baby beet, potato and blue cheese salad p40
Warm goat's cheese on a green bean, watercress and hazelnut salad p42

CHICKEN

Chicken faggots p138
Chicken lasagne p140
Corn-fed chicken, French-style peas, potato wafer and chicken gravy p146
Grilled chicken breast with summer vegetable salad p152
Lemon and thyme chicken kebabs p182
Paprika chicken legs on roast tomatoes p188
Pressed smoked chicken with piccalilli p168
Roast chicken, pea and potato soup p74

Roast crown of chicken with Indian spices, red and yellow peppers and courgettes, basmati rice and curry essence p164
Smoked chicken, bacon and ginger soup p82
Spiced chicken koftas with sesame seed and parsley dressing p190
Salad of breast of chicken with avocado, cherry tomatoes and herb dressing p30

CHILLI

Roast chilli butternut squash and tomato soup p78

COCKLES

Gazpacho with cockles p54

COCONUT

Avocado and coconut soup p46
Coconut rice pudding with Nigel's jam p206
Mango and coconut pancakes p214

COFFEE

Apple meringue crumble with coffee custard p200

COTTAGE PIE

Cauliflower cheese cottage pie p136
Mustard crust cottage pie p158

COURGETTE

Pea, courgette, cucumber, spring onion and asparagus salad, on little gem leaf with a radish dressing p26
Roast crown of chicken with Indian spices, red and yellow peppers and courgettes, basmati rice and curry essence p164
Tuna steaks on courgettes with chermoula p196

CUCUMBER

Chilled cucumber and green pepper soup p50

CURRY

Roast crown of chicken with Indian spices, red and yellow peppers and courgettes, basmati rice and curry essence p164

CUSTARD

Apple meringue crumble with coffee custard p200

Acknowledgements

This book has been a real team effort and put together amazingly quickly thanks to so many people. The team at Buckingham Book Publishing Katy, Phil, Sue..... must have dreaded hearing my voice as we made all the changes that made this book what it is, thanks go to them. A great big thank you to Myburgh and his assistant Charlotte for the brilliant photography all achieved so quickly and to all at Brocket Hall, Michel Roux, Diego and his team at The Waterside Inn and to the management of Butlins Bognor Regis for helping and being so understanding as we used their great venues for our pictures. Whilst on the subject of Butlins at Bognor, rolls off the tongue doesn't it? I must say thanks to Jeremy Pardey and Freddy Hassan for their hard work in getting everything
I needed sorted out so quickly and a special thanks to the head chef at Butlins Bognor Nigel Davis. Nigel is a man I have known for years and is an exceptionally skilled cook and like me a lover of good simple food. The kitchen team at Bognor are fab, hardworking guys and thanks to every one of you, you did a sterling job. As did Nigel Tolley in supplying the superb crockery from Steelite International.

So last but not least to Peter Marshall whose drive sent us all mad but whose determination got us there, thanks Peter.

Oh I mustn't forget Louise, my director, organiser and general factotum, making sure I had what I needed when I needed it, that I was where I should have been at the right time and that I was in the kitchen to cook these fab dishes. But me in the kitchen wasn't enough, I had the help of Gerard O'Sullivan and George Whitelock, thanks especially to Gerard the most hard working, food loving cook I have ever had standing by my side at the stove. Gerard is an inspiration and I thank him as well as all the others for their help – Ta!!!